United States
Department of
Agriculture

Forest Service

Pacific Northwest
Research Station

General Technical
Report
PNW-GTR-598
April 2004

Silvicultural Options for Young-Growth Douglas-Fir Forests: The Capitol Forest Study— Establishment and First Results

Editors   **Robert O. Curtis**, emeritus scientist, **David D. Marshall**, research forester, and **Dean S. DeBell**, (retired), Forestry Sciences Laboratory, 3625-93rd Avenue SW, Olympia, WA 98512-9193.

Silvicultural Options for Young-Growth Douglas-Fir Forests: The Capitol Forest Study—Establishment and First Results

Robert O. Curtis, David D. Marshall, and Dean S. DeBell, Editors

U.S. Department of Agriculture, Forest Service
Pacific Northwest Research Station
Portland, Oregon
General Technical Report PNW-GTR-598
April 2004

Contributors

Kamal M. Ahmed, research associate, University of Washington, Department of Civil and Environmental Engineering, Box 352700, Seattle, WA 98195-2700

Hans Andersen, Ph.D. candidate, University of Washington, College of Forest Resources, Box 352112, Seattle, WA 98195-3112

Gordon A. Bradley, professor, University of Washington, College of Forest Resources, Box 352112, Seattle, WA 98195-3112

Leslie C. Brodie, forester, U.S. Department of Agriculture, Forest Service, Pacific Northwest Research Station, Forestry Sciences Laboratory, 3625-93rd Avenue SW, Olympia, WA 98512-9193

Andrew B. Carey, wildlife biologist, U.S. Department of Agriculture, Forest Service, Pacific Northwest Research Station, Forestry Sciences Laboratory, 3625-93rd Avenue SW, Olympia, WA 98512-9193

Robert O. Curtis, emeritus scientist, U.S. Department of Agriculture, Forest Service, Pacific Northwest Research Station, Forestry Sciences Laboratory, 3625-93rd Avenue SW, Olympia, WA 98512-9193

Terry A. Curtis, photogrammetry supervisor, forester, Washington Department of Natural Resources, Olympia, WA 98501

Dean S. DeBell, (retired), U.S. Department of Agriculture, Forest Service, Pacific Northwest Research Station, Forestry Sciences Laboratory, 3625-93rd Avenue SW, Olympia, WA 98512-9193

Jeffrey D. DeBell, forester, Washington Department of Natural Resources, Olympia, WA 98501

Bruce A. Haveri, biological technician, U.S. Department of Agriculture, Forest Service, Pacific Northwest Research Station, Forestry Sciences Laboratory, 3625-93rd Avenue SW, Olympia, WA 98512-9193

Leonard R. Johnson, professor, University of Idaho, College of Natural Resources, Moscow, ID, 83844-1135

Anne R. Kearney, research assistant professor, University of Washington, College of Forest Resources, Box 352112, Seattle, WA 98195-3112

John F. Klepac, engineer, U.S. Department of Agriculture, Forest Service, Southern Research Station, Andrews Forestry Sciences Laboratory, 520 DeVall Drive, Auburn, AL 36849

Bruce R. Lippke, professor, University of Washington, College of Forest Resources, Box 352112, Seattle, WA 98195-3112

Michelle Ludwig, graduate student, University of Washington, College of Forest Resources, Box 352112, Seattle, WA 98195-3112

David D. Marshall, research forester, U.S. Department of Agriculture, Forest Service, Pacific Northwest Research Station, Forestry Sciences Laboratory, 3625-93rd Avenue SW, Olympia, WA 98512-9193

David Peter, ecologist, U.S. Department of Agriculture, Forest Service, Pacific Northwest Research Station, Forestry Sciences Laboratory, 3625-93rd Avenue SW, Olympia, WA 98512-9193

Stephen E. Reutebuch, research forester, U.S. Department of Agricultre, Forest Service, Pacific Northwest Research Station, Forestry Sciences Laboratory, 3625-93rd Avenue SW, Olympia, WA 98512-9193

Scott Robinson, forester, Washington Department of Natural Resources, Olympia, WA 98501

John Shumway, former soil scientist, U.S. Department of Agriculture, Forest Service, Pacific Northwest Research Station, Forestry Sciences Laboratory, 3625-93rd Avenue SW, Olympia, WA 98512-9193

J. Alan Wagar, research professor, University of Washington, College of Forest Resources, Box 352112, Seattle, WA 98195-3112

Todd M. Wilson, wildlife biologist, U.S. Department of Agriculture, Forest Service, Pacific Northwest Research Station, Forestry Sciences Laboratory, 3625-93rd Avenue SW, Olympia, WA 98512-9193

Kevin Zobrist, economic analyst, University of Washington, College of Forest Resources, Box 352112, Seattle, WA 98195-3112

Summary

Descriptive statistics and some initial results are presented for an operation-scale study being conducted by Pacific Northwest Research Station and the Washington Department of Natural Resources in cooperation with the University of Washington and University of Idaho. The study compares a number of widely different silvicultural regimes applied to young-growth Douglas-fir (*Pseudotsuga menziesii* (Mirb.) Franco) stands in western Washington managed for multiple objectives. The first replicate was established in 1997-98. A second replicate was harvested in the summer of 2002 and a third is planned for 2004.

The regimes compared are (1) conventional clearcutting, (2) retention of reserve trees to create a two-age stand, (3) small patch cuts dispersed within a thinned matrix, repeated at approximately 15-year intervals to create a mosaic of age classes, (4) group selection within a thinned matrix on an approximate 15-year cycle, (5) repeated thinning on an extended rotation, and (6) an extended rotation on an untreated control. Variables to be evaluated include timber growth and yield, regeneration, harvest costs, sale layout and administration costs, public acceptance, soil disturbance, bird populations, and economics.

We have no growth data as yet, but some preliminary results are available for other aspects of the study.

- Windfall losses in the first 4 years after establishment were comparatively small, occurring mainly in the two-age and patch cut units and around the margins of the clearcut unit.

- Sale preparation costs were lowest for the clearcut and highest for group selection. Costs per acre for the repeated thinning, two-age, and patch cut regimes were similar. Cost per unit of volume decreased, however, as volume removed increased. A major element in costs was cost of marking, which could be considerably reduced in the future.

- Harvesting was with ground-based equipment. The clearcut unit had the lowest harvesting cost per thousand board feet. The two-age regime was about 9 percent higher, the patch cut was 17 percent higher, group selection 16 percent higher, and thinning 24 percent higher than the clearcut cost.

- Soil surface disturbance was evaluated on a series of transects. In general, as removal intensity increased the percentage of disturbed area increased (22.5 to 32.2 percent). There was little rutting on any of the units.

- Photographs of the several treatments were used in a preference survey administered to several user groups. All groups showed a preference for "green natural appearance," and foresters tended to be more accepting of visible harvesting activity. Although group preferences were generally similar in direction of preference, environmentalists and foresters tended to be at the extremes, with other groups in the middle.

- Economic returns were compared on the basis of simulation projections of the present stands and present net value of estimated timber yields. The order of present net values by regimes was clearcut > two-age > patch cut > group selection > continued thinning. The estimates do not consider the associated nonmonetary values, or the effects of different rotation options, and also involve somewhat uncertain assumptions about edge effects and growth of trees in small groups. They do give an indication of the costs involved in modifying management to meet nontimber objectives.

- A spring bird survey was conducted following completion of harvest. Both abundance and species richness appeared to decline relative to control in the treatments with greatest disturbance. There were also differences among species in abundance by treatment.

- Because it provided detailed stand information on a grid of plots of precisely known location, the experimental area was used as a test area in an evaluation of laser light detection and ranging (LIDAR).

The first replication (Blue Ridge) of this study has provided valuable information on the establishment of several untested and undocumented regimes in coastal Douglas-fir. As these stands develop following initial treatment, quantitative data will become available on the changes that are expected in habitat structure within treatments and associated bird use, change in visual preferences, and tree growth and survival. The first replicate has already had major educational value as the site of many tours by foresters, students, and user groups. In the future, data from these studies should provide managers with quantitative data needed for informed decisions on selection of regimes suitable for given situations.

Abstract

Curtis, Robert O.; Marshall, David D.; DeBell, Dean S., eds. 2004. Silvicultural options for young-growth Douglas-fir forests: the Capitol Forest study—establishment and first results. Gen. Tech. Rep. PNW-GTR-598. Portland, OR: U.S. Department of Agriculture, Forest Service, Pacific Northwest Research Station. 110 p.

This report describes the origin, design, establishment and measurement procedures and first results of a large long-term cooperative study comparing a number of widely different silvicultural regimes applied to young-growth Douglas-fir (*Pseudotsuga menziesii*) stands managed for multiple objectives. Regimes consist of (1) conventional clearcutting followed by intermediate thinning; (2) retention of reserve trees to create a two-aged stand; (3) small patch cuts dispersed within a thinned matrix, repeated at approximately 15-year intervals to create a mosaic of age classes; (4) group selection within a thinned matrix on an approximate 15-year cycle; (5) continued thinning on an extended rotation; and (6) an untreated control. Each of these regimes is on operation-size units (about 30 to 70 acres each). Output variables to be evaluated include conventional timber growth and yield statistics, harvest costs, sale layout and administration costs, aesthetic effects and public acceptance, soil disturbance, bird populations, and economic aspects. Descriptive statistics and some initial results are presented for the first replicate, established in 1997-98.

Keywords: Silvicultural systems, multiple use, ecosystem management, landscape management, forest ecology, aesthetics, *Pseudotsuga menziesii*.

Contents

Chapter 1: Introduction

Robert O. Curtis, David D. Marshall, and Dean S. DeBell

Silviculturists of the Olympia Forestry Sciences Laboratory, Pacific Northwest Research Station, have joined with foresters of the Washington State Department of Natural Resources and scientists of University of Washington and University of Idaho to establish a long-term comparison of silvicultural regimes for regeneration and management of young-growth Douglas-fir (*Pseudotsuga menziesii* (Mirb.) Franco) forests.

In this report we review the concerns that led to the study, the study design and methodology, and expected expansion over the next few years. We document establishment of the first replicate (Blue Ridge) of the study, and we give some initial results based on the first several years of work at that installation.

The Douglas-fir region of western Washington and northwestern Oregon contains some of the most productive forest land in the Nation and in the world. Fifty-three percent of the unreserved (as of 1987) forest land is capable of growing more than 120 $ft^3 \cdot acre^{-1} \cdot yr^{-1}$ and 80 percent of the land more than 85 $ft^3 \cdot acre^{-1} \cdot yr^{-1}$ (from tables 4 and 5 in Waddel and others 1989). In contrast, the comparable national figures for forest land exclusive of the Douglas-fir region are only 6 percent over 120 $ft^3 \cdot acre^{-1} \cdot yr^{-1}$ and 23 percent over 85 $ft^3 \cdot acre^{-1} \cdot yr^{-1}$. Forest products dominated the region's economy until recently, and they are still very important although now a smaller fraction of the economy.

Beginning with establishment of a large-scale timber industry in the mid-1800s, and through the early 1900s, the prevailing harvest practice was simple liquidation. After unsatisfactory experience with the scattered seed tree method and selective cutting, by the 1940s managers widely adopted a system of dispersed clearcuts with natural regeneration after slash burning. In the 1950s, planting replaced natural regeneration as a quicker and more reliable method. Clearcut, burn, and plant became the standard and almost the only practice. Planting eliminated the need to reserve seed blocks, and many owners adopted large clearcuts to reduce logging, transportation, regeneration, and administration costs. Concurrently, there was a progressive reduction in rotation ages on the part of many owners.

These practices produced landscapes having a considerable part of the area in an unsightly recently harvested condition, and the rest in uniform dense stands that are not particularly attractive visually and that are the least productive habitat for many species of wildlife.

There were associated social changes. Prior to World War II, much of the Northwest population lived in rural and small town settings and had direct contact with practical land management. People in these settings tended to take a utilitarian view of forests. But after the war, there was a huge influx of people from other parts of the country. Most came from urban backgrounds and knew little about Northwest history or Northwest forests. The region was urbanizing, and its economy was changing and becoming less directly dependent on natural resources. Much of the population came to view forests primarily as scenic, wildlife, and recreational areas, with little understanding of the forests' history and dynamic nature, the reasons for the management operations they observed, or the range of possible management options. Some viewed harvest operations as forest destruction.

The combination of these factors has produced increasing polarization and conflict between individuals and institutions concerned with the economic needs for commodity production from forests and those primarily interested in their amenity, environmental, and wildlife values. We believe these conflicts and their consequences for land management policies constitute the most critical problem in Northwestern forestry today. There is a great need for management regimes that can reduce conflicts while providing for integrated production of the many values associated with forests, including the timber harvests that can directly or indirectly finance the provision of other values.

Silviculturists have long recognized a need to develop and evaluate a range of management regimes (silvicultural systems) to meet multiple objectives in managed forests. A wide variety of silvicultural systems has been used elsewhere in the world, but the prevailing system in the Pacific Northwest and the only one for which we have good information on costs, implementation techniques, and consequences is the clearcutting system with either natural or artificial regeneration and with or without intermediate thinning.

Many organizations are now trying different approaches in attempts to satisfy various combinations of owner objectives, societal expectations, and regulatory requirements. But, most such efforts have not been designed in a way that will allow quantitative determination of gains or losses in comparison with conventional clearcutting, or even whether the desired objectives are being attained. Although in recent years a number of experiments have been established that compare effects of alternative harvest practices applied at one point in time, we have as yet no examples in the coastal Douglas-fir region of silvicultural systems other than clearcutting that have been systematically applied over a long period with the design and data collection procedures necessary to make sound quantitative comparisons of their biological, financial, and social consequences.

Reference

Waddell, K.L.; Oswald, D.D.; Powell, D.S. 1989. Forest statistics of the United States, 1987. Resour. Bull. PNW-RB-168. Portland, OR: U.S. Department of Agriculture, Forest Service, Pacific Northwest Research Station. 106 p.

Chapter 2: The Silvicultural Options Study

Robert O. Curtis, Dean S. DeBell, and Jeffrey D. DeBell

Introduction

The Washington Department of Natural Resources (DNR) administers some 2.1 million acres of state forest land, much of it in the highly productive west-side Douglas-fir region. The primary objective—defined by law—is to generate income in perpetuity for trust beneficiaries consisting of educational and other state and county institutions. The DNR also must retain broad citizen support. Public concerns stemming from the visual effects of harvesting activities have become major considerations in DNR management decisions, especially along major travel routes. There is a need for sound quantitative information about the consequences of alternative practices in terms of public response to visual appearance, economic costs and returns, and the associated biological and ecological effects.

The Pacific Northwest Research Station (PNW), DNR, University of Washington, and University of Idaho scientists are cooperating in an operation-scale study that compares harvest and regeneration options. This study is located on the Capitol State Forest, a 90,000-acre forest near Olympia, Washington, managed by DNR. Douglas-fir (*Pseudotsuga menziesii* (Mirb.) Franco) is the predominant species although some western hemlock (*Tsuga heterophylla* (Raf.) Sarg.), western redcedar (*Thuja plicata* Donn ex D. Don), and red alder (*Alnus rubra* Bong.) are present. Many stands are 50 to 70 years old and would normally be considered ready for regeneration harvest, but DNR plans to defer harvest of some in order to develop a more balanced age distribution. The forest contains and abuts many scenic areas and is adjoined by many residences, and portions are visible from major travel routes. Much of the forest is surrounded by industrial lands where extensive recent cutting indirectly limits DNR options.

Literature Review

There is a large body of literature dealing with techniques of natural and artificial regeneration of Douglas-fir under the clearcutting system and with intermediate management of the resulting even-aged stands, and good yield estimates for such management are available. Until recently, most of this work was in the context of a primary objective of timber production.

There have been a few experiments with shelterwood cutting, mostly in mature or old-growth stands (e.g., Williamson 1973, Williamson and Ruth 1975).

The early and unsuccessful work with selective cutting (Curtis 1998, Isaac 1956, Kirkland and Brandstrom 1936) was done in old-growth stands under unfavorable economic conditions and has little relevance to management of young-growth stands.

There has been considerable work on alternative systems in other regions and types (Dale et al. 1995, Leak 1999, Leak and Filip 1977, Marquis 1981, Miller and Schuler 1995, Miller et al. 1995, Smith et al. 1989). These authors have reported on various forms of group selection, small patch cuts, and two-age management as means of mitigating visual impacts of forestry operations and improving wildlife habitat while maintaining timber production.

Evaluation of visual impacts and economic and wildlife aspects requires fairly large experimental units. Several large experiments comparing alternative silvicultural systems on operation-size units that were established in the Northeast during the 1950s (e.g., Sendak et al. 2003) have considerable similarities to the study described in this report. Baker (1994) described a very large-scale recently established interdisciplinary study addressing similar questions in the Ouachita Mountains of Arkansas.

Early work on reproductive requirements of Douglas-fir (Isaac 1943) showed that successful establishment and early growth of Douglas-fir on mesic sites generally require openings of 1 acre or more or overstory densities of less than 50 percent of full stocking. Current work on Oregon State University's McDonald Forest found satisfactory initial establishment under residual overstories of 8 to 12 trees per acre and on small patch cuts of 0.5 acre (Ketchum and Tappeiner, in press). Brandeis (1999) found markedly reduced survival and early growth of Douglas-fir planted under residual overstories of 75, 85, 112, and 128 ft²/acre basal area.

It has become apparent that many questions relating to integrated management for multiple resource objectives cannot be answered by the type of small-plot silvicultural studies common in the past. These questions require long-term experimentation on areas large enough to allow evaluation of operational feasibility, public response to visual effects, wildlife effects, comparative costs, and timber yields (McComb et al. 1994).

Several large-scale experiments involving different forms of nonstandard silviculture recently have been established in the Pacific Northwest (Monserud 2002). Perhaps the most elaborate of these is the Demonstration of Ecosystems Options (DEMO) study (Franklin et al. 1999). In that study, however, most installations are in mature stands, stand treatments are confined to a single entry and do not include the subsequent operations that most managers consider essential in a management regime having timber production as one of its major objectives, and comparative cost data are lacking.

Curtis et al. (1998), DeBell and Curtis (1993), DeBell et al. (1998), Curtis and Carey (1996), and Kohm and Franklin (1997) have discussed possible practices for integrated production of both timber and other forest values in the Douglas-fir region. The study reported here is a further development of these ideas.

Objectives

This experiment is intended to provide a comparison of silvicultural regimes that will have long-term value both for research and demonstration. The selected silvicultural regimes are planned programs of silvicultural treatment extending over the entire life of the stand, from regeneration through intermediate operations to final harvest and regeneration. The objectives are:

- To create on-the-ground examples of a number of contrasting silvicultural regimes that can be evaluated for effectiveness in reducing visual and other environmental impacts of forestry operations while providing high timber outputs over time.

- To monitor development of stands under these contrasting regimes over an extended period by using procedures that will provide quantitative estimates of biological and physical change, timber outputs, costs, and statistically sound tests of differences between regimes.

Design Considerations

Early in the project, PNW scientists and DNR managers agreed on several principles that would guide its development.

Joint Design by Managers and Scientists

Local managers and field foresters identified the driving issue: develop harvesting options that reconcile aesthetic values with economic return and sustained wood production in visually sensitive areas. Research scientists provided guidance in experimental design. Together, we developed (a) rational regimes (silvicultural systems), (b) ways to implement and test them, and (3) methods to obtain the quantitative data needed for useful comparisons.

Operational and Adaptive Nature

Operational scale and operational feasibility were essential if the project was to provide useful information to managers and be effective as a demonstration area. We agreed that in each option we would carry out whatever intermediate operations were necessary to provide the desired regeneration and stand structure. Thus, a given cultural practice (e.g., herbicide application, animal damage control) might be necessary for some regimes or sites but not for others, and the associated costs and complications become part of the evaluation.

Financial and Staffing Resources

No special funding was initially available to either organization. Stand treatments were to be done as components of ongoing operations in conjunction with DNR's timber sale program. Evaluation procedures were planned so that much basic data on stand growth and development could be collected within the framework of existing PNW funding, although we hope to attract additional partners and funds for assessment of other biological and social values.

Continuity—Any project comparing silvicultural regimes must continue beyond the careers of the initial participants. We attempted to incorporate a number of features to favor long-term survival and continuity:

1. Wide range of options: Social needs and desires change as do forest conditions. Even in multipurpose forests, the relative importance of different features will no doubt differ 20 or more years hence.

2. Large treatment areas and adequate replication: Size and number of treatment areas must be sufficient to accommodate the damage and mortality that are to be expected on any operational unit and still provide useful information. Also, assessments of nontimber values such as wildlife habitat generally require larger areas than assessments of timber values alone.

3. Applicability to major portions of the forest land base: The areas selected must be representative of major portions of the land base available for multipurpose forestry.

4. Minimum essential expenses: Essential expenses should be minimized so that the project can survive the lows of financial cycles and political interest. Flexibility should be provided to accommodate additional work when resources permit.

5. Multiple disciplines and organizations: Inclusion of multiple disciplines and cooperating organizations can increase cost efficiency and permit more comprehensive evaluations. Diversity in partners can help to buffer the project from the cycles of support that occur within and among disciplines and organization.

Statistical Design

The study is a randomized block design, having six treatments and a minimum of three replicates on Capitol Forest, with possibilities of additional replication at other locations. Stand growth and yield information is based primarily on repeated measurements on a grid of permanent plots, maintained for the life of the experiment. Supplementary short-term studies of aspects such as harvesting costs, visual impacts, and wildlife also are planned and in progress in cooperation with other organizations.

Choice of Regimes

As we use the terms in this report, a silvicultural regime (system) is a planned series of treatments for tending, harvesting, and regenerating a stand. A silvicultural treatment is a single silvicultural operation that is part of a silvicultural regime. A unit is the physical land area to which a specific silvicultural regime is applied.

Limitations imposed by cost, area required for each selected regime, and size of available homogeneous areas meant that only a limited number of possible regimes could be included. We selected six regimes that we expect to (1) produce sharply contrasting stand structures and visual effects and (2) be biologically and operationally feasible on the basis of existing knowledge.

The regimes selected are (1) clearcut, (2) two-age, (3) patch cut, (4) group selection, (5) extended rotation with repeated thinning (hereafter referred to as thinning), and (6) extended rotation without thinning (control). Each regime consists of a sequence of operations applied over an extended period and intended to produce stands with widely different characteristics. Regimes are applied to units of about 30 to 70 acres. We expect differences in economic productivity and public response, but each regime would be reasonable under some circumstances. Four regimes are regeneration harvests; the other two extend the rotation age of the present stand (one with thinning, the other without thinning). These options will lead to even-aged, two-aged, and uneven-aged stands (fig. 2-1), thus creating a wide range of stand conditions, habitat values, and visual appearances. Below, we outline the general characteristics of each regime and intended goal, without attempting to specify in advance the exact nature and timing of all activities needed to achieve this.

Clearcut

This regime is well understood and is included primarily to provide a direct quantitative comparison of clearcut costs and outputs with those of the other regimes discussed.

Initial cut—Cut all merchantable and unmerchantable trees on the area, except for streamside strips and scattered groups of leave trees as needed to meet Forest Practices Act and Habitat Conservation Plan requirements.

Regeneration—Plant according to current DNR practice, predominantly Douglas-fir with western redcedar or possibly some alder in root rot areas.

Subsequent operations—

- Brush control, if and when needed, according to current DNR practice.

- Precommercial thinning, if needed, depending on stocking achieved and feasibility of early commercial thinning as an alternative. Retain some naturally established stems of species other than Douglas-fir, when present.

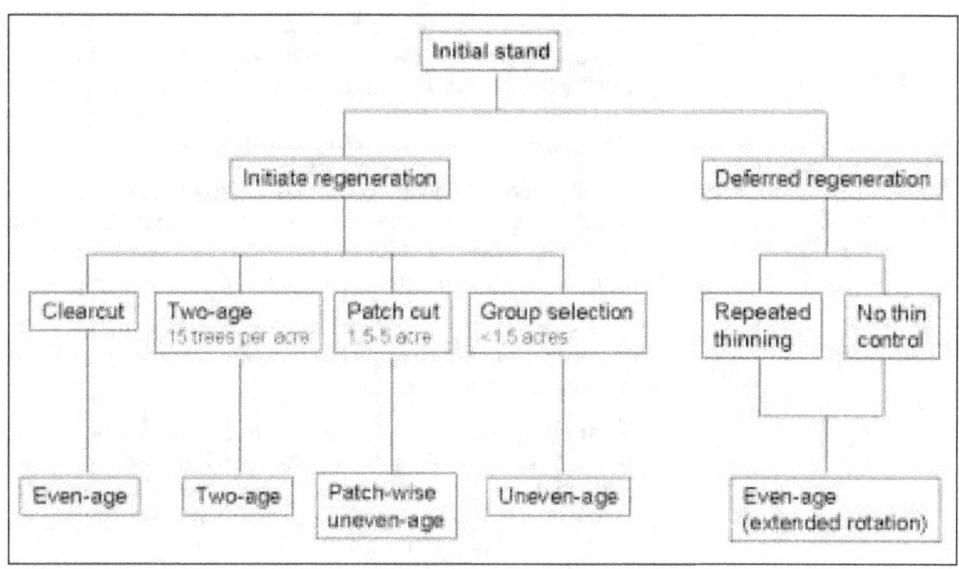

Figure 2-1—Relationships among treatment regimes.

- Commercial thinning as needed, to reduce relative density (RD) (Curtis 1982) to about RD35 in the first thinning and thereafter to maintain density in the range of RD40 to RD60.

- Harvest at a rotation age to be determined, probably in the range of 60 to 80 years.

Characteristics and current expectations—A well-understood and simple regime that will probably maximize timber yield and minimize harvest and administrative costs. Appearance may be objectionable to much of the public.

Two-Age Stand Management (Reserve Shelterwood)

This initially resembles a conventional shelterwood but with the overwood, or a portion of it, carried through the second rotation to provide large trees and high-quality material.

Initial cut—This will remove a high percentage of the initial basal area, with a target residual stand of 15 trees per acre, or about 20 percent of initial basal area. Leave trees will be selected for vigor and stem quality.

Regeneration—Supplement existing and prospective natural regeneration by underplanting with Douglas-fir. The aim is a mixed-species stand including 50 percent or more Douglas-fir.

Subsequent operations—

- Brush control, if and when needed.

- Precommercial thinning some years after initial cut if needed to control spacing and remove damaged advance regeneration.

- Commercial thinning as needed to maintain reasonable growth rates in the younger cohort.

- Remove some overstory trees if and when needed to maintain satisfactory development of understory.

- Harvest at a rotation age to be determined, perhaps 60 years after initial cut.

Characteristics and current expectations—Maintains at least partial forest cover over at least two conventional rotations and sharply reduces the area in the highly visible, freshly harvested condition. Potential for high-value production in the retained overstory. Layered structure favorable to some wildlife. Probable increase in hemlock component. Possibility of major windfall losses. Possible difficulty in marketing very large trees.

Patch Cut (Patch-Wise Uneven-Age) Management

Small patch cuts on the order of 1.5 to 5 acres can be treated by conventional even-age management techniques emphasizing Douglas-fir. Over time, a unit can be converted to an uneven-aged mosaic of even-aged patches that would be predominantly Douglas-fir while lacking large and visually obtrusive harvest areas.

The 1.5-acre minimum patch size is determined by the need for (1) direct light for satisfactory development of Douglas-fir and (2) avoidance of future need to fell large trees into established regeneration.

First entry—Cut all stems on 1.5- to 5-acre patches, somewhat irregular in shape, dispersed over the unit, and amounting to 20 percent of the available area. Concurrently do a light thinning in the intervening areas, aimed to reduce RD in the thinned area to about RD45. Plant patches to Douglas-fir or a mix of Douglas-fir and other species. Do any brush control needed to obtain reasonable survival and early growth.

Subsequent entries (15-year cycle)—Make additional patch cuts and regenerate another 20 percent of the area. Precommercially thin regenerated patches as needed. Commercially thin intervening areas as appropriate. This will, in time, produce a unit consisting of five age classes with a 75-year rotation, a condition that could be maintained indefinitely.

Characteristics and current expectations—Avoids large and highly visible harvest areas, provides near-constant landscapes, will probably maintain Douglas-fir and provide long-term yields near those under clearcutting. Uses well-understood even-age management techniques. Mix of habitat conditions should be favorable for many wildlife species. Harvest and administrative costs may be higher than under the clearcut and two-age regimes. Increased amount of edge may result in windfall losses higher than in the clearcut regime.

Because of the extended conversion period involved in this and in the group selection regime (below), the initial cut in these regimes should ideally be made at younger ages that the 70-year-old stands used in the first replicate of this study. Future replicates should include younger stands.

Group Selection

This resembles the patch cut regime (above), except that removals will cover a range from individual trees to groups not exceeding 1.5 acres, on the same 15-year cycle. Residual basal area over the unit will be comparable to that of the patch cut regime of the same replication. Early entries will not differ much from conventional thinning except for conscious creation of scattered openings intended to secure or release regeneration.

Openings of 0.1 acre and larger will be planted to Douglas-fir. Brush control and precommercial thinning will be done in openings as needed to ensure survival and development of regeneration.

Characteristics and current expectations—Compared to the patch cut regime, smaller group sizes mean (a) reduced visual impacts, (b) increased difficulty in managing intermediate treatments, and (c) increased harvest cost and damage. The small size of openings will probably result in reduced representation of Douglas-fir in regeneration and possibly in reduced growth of all species.

Extended Rotation With Repeated Thinning

Available information suggests that systematic thinning of vigorous Douglas-fir stands can maintain high growth rates in volume and value for extended periods, well beyond commonly used rotations. Continued commercial thinning can prolong the period of high production and produce current income while also producing aesthetically desirable and high-value large trees and reducing the land area in highly visible regeneration stages at any point in time. It is, therefore, one of the options to be considered for reducing visual impacts.

The stand would ultimately be reproduced by clearcut, shelterwood, or patch cut methods, at some rotation age now unspecified.

Extended Rotation Without Thinning (Control)

This provides a comparison with gains obtainable by the repeated thinning regime (above) when some stands are held on an extended rotation as a means of adjusting currently unbalanced age distributions and reducing visual impacts on the landscape.

Selection of Study Areas

One replicate (block) in this study requires an area of 200 to 250 acres, as nearly uniform in stand characteristics, site, and topography as reasonably attainable. Individual regimes require units of 25 to 50 or more acres, with the less uniform regimes (patch and group cuts) requiring larger areas than the more uniform regimes. To allow randomization of regime assignments, however, areas of 40 to 50 acres should be available for each regime, even though all may not be used. It is desirable, but not essential, that regime areas be contiguous, but they should be in the same general area.

Three replicates are being established on Capitol Forest. The first, Blue Ridge, was cut in 1998, and preharvest and postharvest measurements have been completed. The second, Copper Ridge, was harvested in summer 2002. The third, Rusty Ridge, had plot establishment and initial measurements completed in 2002 and is scheduled to be cut in 2004. The Blue Ridge stand is about 70 years old and originated from natural seeding after cutting and fire, as did Copper Ridge. The Rusty Ridge stand is a plantation and is substantially younger (about 40 years). Blue Ridge and Rusty Ridge are on fairly gentle terrain, and harvesting is by ground-based equipment. Copper Ridge is on much steeper terrain and requires cable logging.

The British Columbia Ministry of Forests has installed an additional replicate on Vancouver Island. Two more are planned.

Measurement Procedures

One major objective is quantitative comparisons of growth and yield among regimes and of the stand structures produced by the different regimes. This requires detailed specification of sampling and measurement procedures that can be applied consistently over long periods and by different people.

The basic stand measurements and procedures are detailed in the study plan.[1]

Stand measurements are based on a systematic grid of permanent 1/5-acre plots. Plots are monumented and trees are identified by tags. Diameters and a sample of heights are measured before cut, after cut, and are repeated on a 5-year cycle thereafter as consistent with planned harvest operations. Regeneration (natural and planted) is inventoried at the same time, with additional regeneration inventories done 1 and 2 years after planting. Planted seedlings are identified. Postharvest regeneration inventories are based on a

---

[1] Curtis, R.O.; Clendenen, G.W.; DeBell, D.S.; DeBell, J.; Poch, T.; Shumway, J. Silvicultural options for harvesting young-growth production forests. Study plan on file at Olympia Forestry Sciences Laboratory. 1997, revised 2001. 34 p.

sample of four 4-milacre plots superimposed on each 1/5-acre permanent plot. Visual estimates of average height and percentage cover of the principal shrub and herbaceous species are recorded.

Time and cost records are kept for all management operations (as opposed to purely research costs) as well as receipts from timber sale and harvest activities, by regime and treatment.

The primary objective is to secure all data necessary for evaluation of comparative production and costs of the different regimes. The supplementary studies discussed below, however, will require collection of additional data specific to the individual study.

Supplementary Studies

A number of supplementary studies are in progress or anticipated. These include evaluations of:

- Harvesting costs

- Public response to visual effects

- Soil effects

- Wildlife effects

- Economics

The extent of these efforts is dependent on funding and cooperative arrangements with other organizations.

The remainder of this report documents the work done to date specifically at the Blue Ridge installation, organized as a number of chapters authored by the individual scientist(s) primarily concerned with each topic. We expect it to be a useful reference for those working on the study in the future, and for visitors seeing the study for the first time.

References

Baker, J.B. 1994. An overview of stand-level ecosystem management research in the Ouachita/Ozark National Forests. In: Baker, J.B., comp. Proceedings, Symposium on ecosystem management research in the Ouachita Mountains: pretreatment condition and preliminary findings. Gen. Tech. Rep. SO-112. Asheville, NC: U.S. Department of Agriculture, Forest Service, Southern Research Station: 18-28.

Brandeis, T.J. 1999. Underplanting and competition in thinned Douglas-fir. Corvallis, OR: Oregon State University. 161 p. Ph.D. dissertation.

Curtis, R.O. 1982. A simple index of stand density for Douglas-fir. Forest Science. 28: 92-94.

Curtis, R.O. 1998. "Selective cutting" in Douglas-fir: history revisited. Journal of Forestry. 96(7): 40-46.

Curtis, R.O.; Carey, A.B. 1996. Timber supply in the Pacific Northwest: managing economic and ecological values in Douglas-fir forests. Journal of Forestry. 94(9): 4-7, 35-37.

Curtis, R.O.; DeBell, D.S.; Harrington, C.A. [et al.]. 1998. Silviculture for multiple objectives in the Douglas-fir region. Gen. Tech. Rep. PNW-GTR-435. Portland, OR: U.S. Department of Agriculture, Forest Service, Pacific Northwest Research Station. 123 p.

Dale, M.E.; Smith, H.C.; Pearcy, J.N. 1995. Size of clearcut openings affects species composition, growth rate, and stand characteristics. Res. Pap. NE-698. Radnor, PA: U.S. Department of Agriculture, Forest Service, Northeastern Forest Experiment Station. 21 p.

DeBell, D.S.; Curtis, R.O. 1993. Silviculture and new forestry in the Pacific Northwest. Journal of Forestry. 91(12): 26-30.

DeBell, D.S.; DeBell, J.D.; Curtis, R.O.; Allison, N.K. 1998. Evaluating and communicating options for harvesting young-growth Douglas-fir forests. In: Communicating the role of silviculture in managing the National Forests: Proceedings of the national silviculture workshop. Gen. Tech. Rep. NE-GTR-238. Radnor, PA: U.S. Department of Agriculture, Forest Service, Northeastern Research Station: 155-162.

Franklin, J.F.; Norris, L.A.; Berg, D.R.; Smith, G.R. 1999. The history of DEMO: an experiment in regeneration harvest of Northwestern forest ecosystems. Northwest Science. 73(Spec. issue): 3-11.

Isaac, L.A. 1943. Reproductive habits of Douglas-fir. Washington, DC: Charles Lathrop Pack Forestry Foundation. 107 p.

Isaac, L.A. 1956. Place of partial cutting in old-growth stands of the Douglas-fir region. Res. Pap. 16. PNW-RP-16. Portland, OR: U.S. Department of Agriculture, Forest Service, Pacific Northwest Forest and Range Experiment Station. 48 p.

Kirkland, B.P.; Branstrom, A.J.F. 1936. Selective timber management in the Douglas-fir region. Washington, DC: U.S. Department of Agriculture, Forest Service. 126 p.

Kohm, K.A.; Franklin, J.F., eds. 1997. Creating a forestry for the 21st century—the science of ecosystem management. Washington, DC: Island Press. 475 p.

Ketchum, J.S.; Tappeiner, J.C. [In press]. Early Douglas-fir, grand fir and plant community responses to three silvicultural treatments (modified clearcut, two-story, and small patch cut). In: Maguire, C.C.; Chambers, C.L., eds. College of forestry integrated research project: ecological and socioeconomic responses to alternative silvicultural treatments. Forestry Research Lab. Publ. 3582. Corvallis, OR: Oregon State University, College of Forestry.

Leak, W.B. 1999. Species composition and structure of a northern hardwood stand after 61 years of group/patch selection. Northern Journal of Applied Forestry. 16(3): 151-153.

Leak, W.B.; Filip, S.M. 1977. Thirty-eight years of group selection in New England northern hardwoods. Journal of Forestry. 75(10): 641-643.

Marquis, D.A. 1981. Hardwood silviculture and management systems: modifications for special objectives. In: Hardwood management: Proceedings of the national silviculture workshop. Washington, DC: U.S. Department of Agriculture, Forest Service, Timber Management: 77-86.

McComb, W.; Tappeiner, J.; Kellogg, L. [et al.]. 1994. Stand management alternatives for multiple resources: integrated management experiments. In: Huff, M.H.; Norris, L.K.; Nyberg, J.B.; Wilkin, N.L., coords. Expanding horizons of forest ecosystem management: Proceedings of the third habitat futures workshop. Gen. Tech. Rep. PNW-GTR-336. Portland, OR: U.S. Department of Agriculture, Forest Service, Pacific Northwest Research Station: 71-86.

Miller, G.W.; Schuler, T.M. 1995. Development and quality of reproduction in two-age central Appalachian hardwoods—10 year results. In: Proceedings, 10th central hardwood forest conference. Gen. Tech. Rep. NE-GTR-197. Radnor, PA: U.S. Department of Agriculture, Forest Service, Northeastern Forest Experiment Station: 364-374.

Miller, G.W.; Wood, P.B.; Nichols, J.V. 1995. Two-age silviculture—an innovative tool for enhancing species diversity and vertical structure in Appalachian hardwoods. In: Eskew, L.G., comp. Forest health through silviculture: Proceedings of the 1995 national silviculture workshop. Gen. Tech. Rep. RM-GTR-267. Fort Collins, CO: U.S. Department of Agriculture, Forest Service, Rocky Mountain Forest and Range Experiment Station: 175-182.

Monserud, R.A. 2002. Large-scale management experiments in the moist maritime forests of the Pacific Northwest. Landscape and Urban Planning. 59: 159-180.

Sendak, P.E.; Brissette, J.C.; Frank, R.M. 2003. Silviculture affects composition, growth, and yield in mixed northern conifers: 40-year results from the Penobscot Experimental Forest. Canadian Journal of Forest Research. 33: 2116-2128.

Smith, H.C.; Lamson, N.I.; Miller, G.W. 1989. An aesthetic alternative to clearcutting? Deferment cutting in eastern hardwoods. Journal of Forestry. 87(3): 14-18.

Williamson, R.L. 1973. Results of shelterwood harvesting of Douglas-fir in the Cascades of western Oregon. Res. Pap. PNW-RP-161. Portland, OR: U.S. Department of Agriculture, Forest Service, Pacific Northwest Forest and Range Experiment Station. 13 p.

Williamson, R.L.; Ruth, R.H. 1975. Results of shelterwood cutting in western hemlock. Res. Pap. PNW-201. Portland, OR: U.S. Department of Agriculture, Forest Service, Pacific Northwest Forest and Range Experiment Station. 25 p.

Chapter 3: Blue Ridge Layout and Stand Measurements

Robert O. Curtis, Dean S. DeBell, David D. Marshall, Jeffrey D. DeBell, and Leslie C. Brodie

This chapter describes the experimental site, the physical arrangement of treatment units and of measurement plots within units, and the silvicultural operations and vegetation measurements carried out from establishment in 1997-98 through 2002.

Location

The Blue Ridge installation, the first block in the Capitol Forest study, is located in sections 22 and 23, T. 16 N, R. 2 W. Topography is quite gentle. Elevation is about 1,100 ft. It is within the high-rainfall (60+ in per year) western portion of Capitol Forest. Soils are Olympic silt clay loam (deep and well-drained from weathered basalt) as shown in generalized maps in *Soil Survey of Thurston County, Washington* (Pringle 1990).[1]

The dominant plant association in all units is TSHE/POMU-OXOR (western hemlock/swordfern-Oregon oxalis).[2] There are also limited inclusions of several other associations, the most important being an area of TSHE/GASH (western hemlock/salal) in the clearcut treatment, TSHE/GASH-BENE2 (western hemlock/salal/Cascade Oregon grape) in the patch cut, and TSHE/GASH/POMU (western hemlock/salal/swordfern) in the two-age, patch cut, and repeated thinning treatments (Henderson et al. 1989).

A site index determination based on the pretreatment measurements indicates an average site index (King 1966) of about 128, a high site II. An immediately adjacent plantation appears to indicate a somewhat higher site index.

Initial Stand

The initial stand was of natural origin, with an estimated date of origin of 1929. Average age from seed was 69 years (as estimated from stumps in 1998), although there is considerable variation in individual tree ages. The area was clearcut and burned sometime in the late 1920s. The 1997 stand was predominantly Douglas-fir (*Pseudotsuga menziesii*

---

[1] A representative Blue Ridge soil profile description by John Shumway is given in appendix 1, soil description at Blue Ridge.

[2] Classification by David Peter, appendix 2, Blue Ridge vegetation assessment.

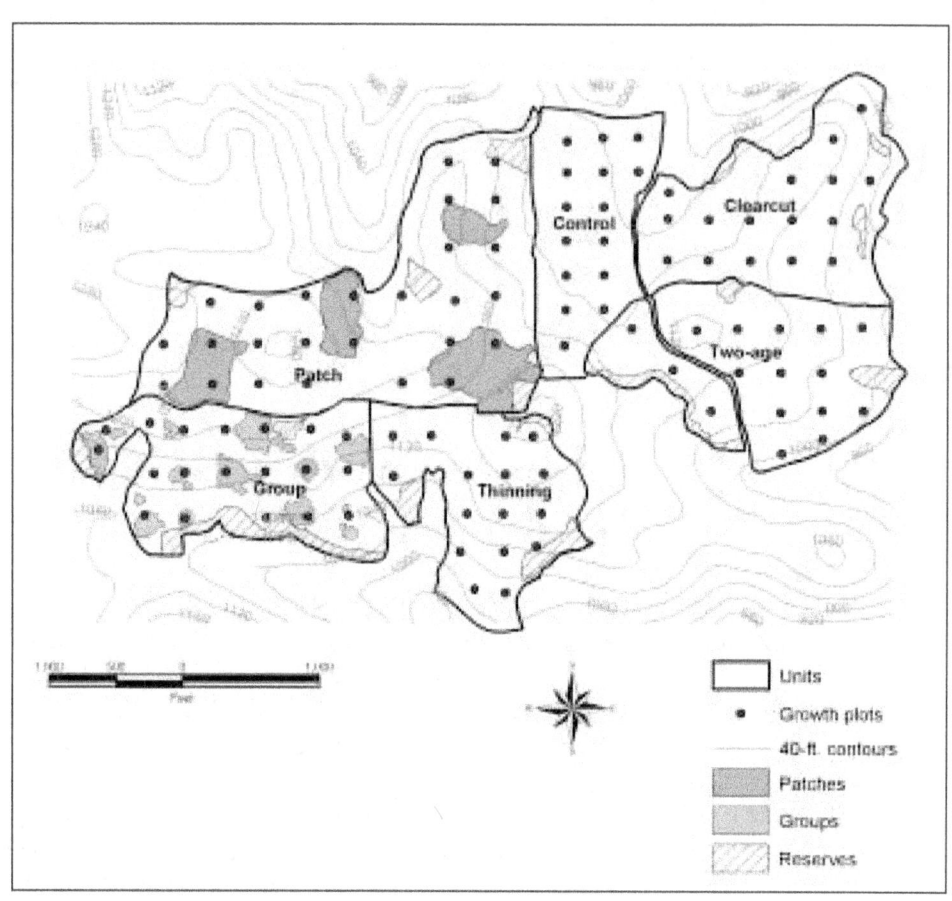

Figure 3-1—Blue ridge installation, plot locations and unit boundaries.

(Mirb.) Franco), with some hemlock (*Tsuga heterophylla* (Raf.) Sarg.), a very small amount of redcedar (*Thuja plicata* Donn ex D. Don), and considerable red alder (*Alnus rubra* Bong.). An ice storm in the winter of 1997 severely damaged the alder but had little effect on the conifers. Most of the area had been thinned in about 1971. Several old portable mill sites date from this thinning and had seeded in to alder.

Terrain is moderate and elevations are about 1,000 to 1,300 ft. Most slopes were in the range of 10 to 30 percent, with occasional slopes to 50 percent. Contours are shown in figure 3-1.

The area is remarkable for a degree of homogeneity in stand conditions unusual in naturally seeded stands without early density control, extending over an area sufficient to accommodate all six regimes. There is little evidence of site differences. This allows contiguous location of regimes and makes this an excellent demonstration area.

Layout of the Experiment (1996-97)

Unit Delineation

The boundaries of the suitable area were roughly delineated by using existing maps, air photos, and limited field reconnaissance. Six equally spaced points were superimposed, and the area subdivided into six more or less equal portions, each centered on one point. The six treatments were randomly assigned to these portions. After assignment, boundaries were expanded or contracted as needed to approximate the desired area for each regime (some, such as the patch cut, require larger areas than others because of the nature of the regime). Unit boundaries drawn on the photos were then flagged on the ground.

Road Layout and Unit Surveys

The Washington Department of Natural Resources (DNR) established access road locations, marked rights-of-way, and handled road construction. Unit boundaries were surveyed jointly by DNR and Pacific Northwest Research Station (PNW), allowing for leave tree clumps and buffers in streamside zones as required by DNR. Final boundaries (after minor changes, below) are shown in figure 3-1. Areas of the silvicultural units, as determined by a combination of photogrammetric measurements and ground survey with global positioning system (GPS) reference points, are shown in table 3-1.

Plot Location

Plots were established in a systematic grid within each regime unit, at spacings designed to produce the desired number of plots for the unit. Because expected variability in growth rates was unknown, number of plots for each regime was a judgment call, with more plots taken in the patch cut and group selection cut than in other more uniform regimes. Plot centers were marked with white plastic pipe and were referenced to three witness trees at each location.

After initial plot location, changes in DNR requirements for streamside buffers and for leave tree clumps required shifting location of a number of plots. These changes are expected to have negligible effect on results but did produce a plot distribution that differs somewhat from the original systematic grid and a slight reduction in the number of plots in the group selection unit. Final locations are shown on map (fig. 3-1). The GPS coordinates for these plots have since been determined.

Pretreatment Plot Measurements (1997)

Pretreatment measurements of all plots were made in late 1996 and early 1997. Tree measurements consisted of species and diameter at breast height (d.b.h., to nearest inch) of all trees on concentric circular plots centered on the plot stake, with a subsample of heights. Trees 1.6 to 5.5 in d.b.h were measured on a central 0.025-acre subplot, trees >5.5 and ≤9.5 in on a concentric 0.10-acre plot, and trees >9.5 in on the full 0.2-acre plot.

Concurrent measurements were made of advance regeneration of tree species on a central 4-milacre plot. Information recorded was (1) height (for trees of height <4.5 ft) or d.b.h (for trees of height >4.5 ft and d.b.h <1.6 in) of the two tallest acceptable seedlings or saplings, and (2) stem count, by species, of trees >1 ft in height and <1.6 in d.b.h.

Percentage cover and average height of each shrub species with more than 10 percent cover were ocularly estimated on a central 0.025-acre subplot.

Marking for Cut (1997)

Based on the initial stand measurements, targets for the residual stand were chosen as follows:

- Clearcut—all trees to be removed except for designated green tree retention groups as required by DNR standards.

- Two-age—15 uniformly distributed trees per acre, except for designated reserve groups.

- Patch cut—20 percent of area to be in cut patches ranging from 1.5 to 5.0 acres. Remainder to be comparable to the repeated thinning treatment.

- Group selection—average residual stocking (basal area) to be roughly comparable to that in the patch unit.

Table 3-1—Unit (treatment) areas in the Blue Ridge installation

Treatment	Excluding new roads and reserves	Reserves	New roads	Total including roads and reserves
	Acres			
Clearcut	40.5	1.3	0	45.5
Two-age	43.1 (42.9)[a]	3.9	0	47
Patch cut	71.8	3.8	5.5	81.1
Group selection	37.7	5.3	1.4	44.4
Repeated thinning	32.9 (32.6)	3.1	1.7	37.7
Control	31.6	0	0	31.6

[a] Values in parentheses are areas remaining after new road construction in 2001.

- Repeated thinning—residual stand to be in the range 160 to 180 ft²/acre, except for designated reserve groups. Cutting primarily from below, with removal of some larger trees of poor stem quality, vigor, or spacing.

- Control—no cutting.

The units were marked for cutting in late summer and early fall 1997, by DNR personnel with some assistance from PNW. Leave trees were marked in the two-age treatment. In patch and group selection, the units were first marked for thinning, and cut patches or groups were then superimposed on the prior marking, with all trees to be cut being marked. The DNR designated patch boundaries and skid trail locations. (Some of these had to be modified later to allow for efficient equipment operation.) Sale preparation costs, including marking, are given in chapter 4.

Harvesting operations were carried out during 1998 and are discussed in chapter 5. Locations of patches and groups in the patch cut and group selection regimes are shown in figure 3-2.

Planting

The cut areas were planted in February 1999, at nominal 10 by 10 ft spacing. Stock was primarily Douglas-fir bareroot 1-1, plus a limited amount of western redcedar plug 1 in root rot areas. Areas planted consisted of (1) clearcut, (2) two-age, (3) cut patches within the patch cut unit, and (4) openings of 0.10 acre and larger in the group selection unit.

These areas were planted by the Cedar Creek Corrections Camp crew. Costs are summarized in table 3-2.

Posttreatment Plot Measurements (Late 1998 to Early 1999)

Stand Age

Ring counts were made on the first sound Douglas-fir stump encountered on each plot that was obviously a dominant or strong codominant, proceeding clockwise from north. Mean across all units was 66.25 rings at stump. Mean stump height was 1.3 ft. Assuming 3 years from seed to stump height and 3 years from stump height to breast height, this gives estimates of 69 years total age and 63 years age at breast height in 1998. There was considerable variation in individual tree age counts (standard deviation of 5.8), indicating that the stand seeded in over a period of some years.

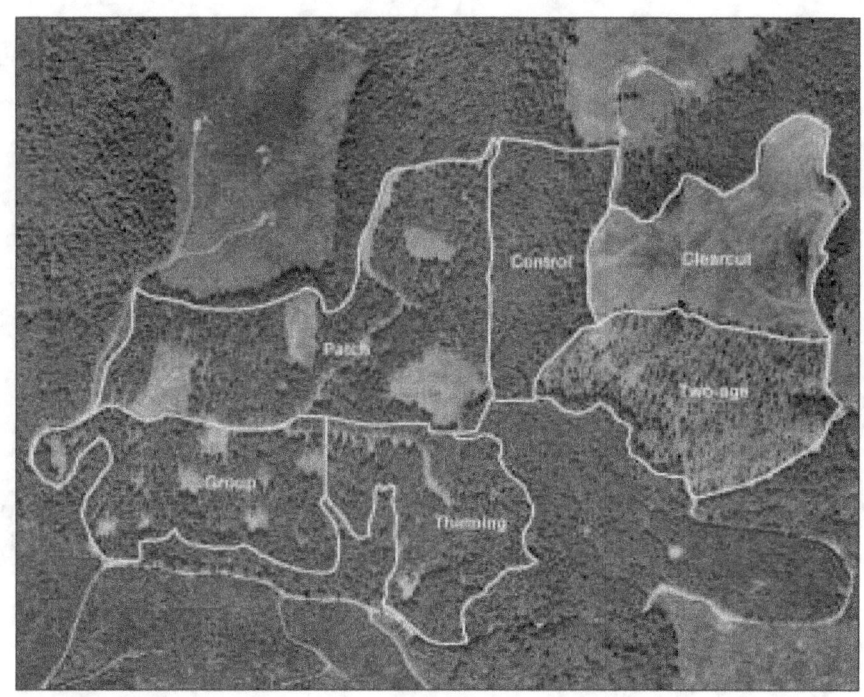

Figure 3-2—Aerial photo after 1998 harvest, showing locations of treatments.

Table 3-2—Planting costs at the Blue Ridge installation

Treatment	Area planted	Labor[a]	Labor[b]	Planting stock	Labor
	Acres	Dollars	Hours	Dollars	Hours per acre
Clearcut	40.5	1,969	446.5	5,133	11.0
Two-age	43.1	1,876	457	5,502	10.6
Patch cut	17.0	788	201.5	2,664	11.8
Group selection	7.6[c]	653	144	1,993	18.9

[a] Prison wage rates, unrealistically low.

[b] Includes crew and foreman.

[c] Does not include area in groups less than 0.1 acre.

Tree measurements—Posttreatment tree figure measurement procedures were similar to the pretreatment measurements, with the following changes (fig. 3-3):

- Each tree was numbered and tagged, proceeding clockwise from north.

- The plot was divided into quadrants and tree tally subdivided accordingly.

- Diameters were recorded to 0.1 inch.

- In patch cut and group selection units, each plot and each quadrant were classified as in patch, not in patch, or overlap.

- Trees were classified by condition, and damage was recorded.

- Snags were recorded.

- The subsample of heights was increased.

Per acre stand statistics were calculated from these values, including basal area, number of trees, cubic and Scribner volumes, and Douglas-fir H40 (mean height of the largest 40 trees per acre) values. Separate height-diameter equations for each treatment were used for Douglas-fir. Height samples were combined across treatments for each of the other species and height-diameter equations were fit separately for western hemlock, redcedar, and alder.

Regeneration

Regeneration measurements were made in spring 1999 and again in spring 2000 by using procedures similar to those in the pretreatment measurements, with the following changes:

- Subsampling was changed to four 4-milacre subplots per main plot, located at the intersections of the plot periphery with east-west and north-south lines through plot center. These were permanently identified with plastic pipe, referenced to the main plot center.

- All planted seedlings on these plots were identified in the record by distance and azimuth from the subplot center.

Understory Vegetation

The intent was to make posttreatment measurements as in the pretreatment measurement, except that four 0.025-acre subplots were to be used per main plot, centered on the regeneration subplot stakes. The first posttreatment remeasurement was missed at Blue Ridge, but in the future will be done at the same time as subsequent regeneration plot measurements.

Stand Characteristics

The stand had been established by natural seeding after clearcut logging and burning, and there is considerable variation in individual tree ages. In general, the pretreatment stand was vigorous and relatively little affected by damaging agents. As noted earlier, most of the area had been thinned about 1971 and it had not reached excessively high densities by 1998, although another thinning was clearly reasonable. Scattered pockets of root rot were present but did not affect a large proportion of the area. An ice storm in winter 1997-98 caused severe stem breakage in the alder but had relatively little effect on the conifers. There was one area of severe dwarf mistletoe (*Arceuthobium* sp.) damage to hemlock, located in the southeast corner of the patch cut unit; this was removed as one of the patches cut in 1998.

Based on the 1997-98 plot measurements, pretreatment basal area distribution (1997) was Douglas-fir 80 percent, western hemlock 15 percent, western redcedar 1 percent, and red alder 4 percent.

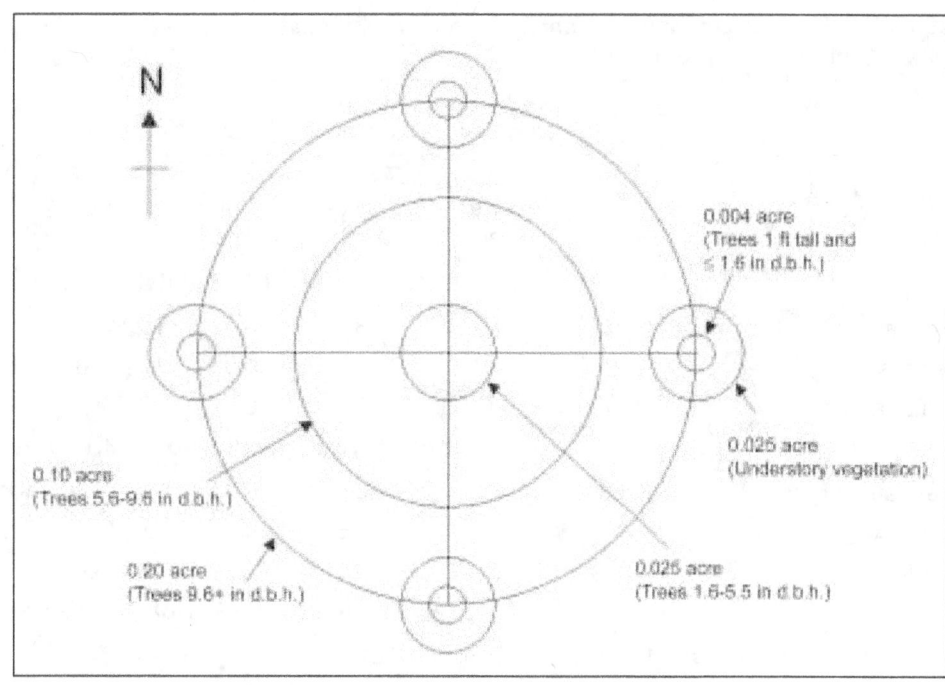

Figure 3-3—Permanent plot design, with associated subplots.

Other pretreatment statistics for area as a whole follow (for trees 5.6 in and larger):

Trees per acre	105.6
Basal area (ft^2/acre)	227.5
QMD (quadratic mean diameter, in)	19.9
Merchantable ft^3/acre (6-in top)	10,715
Board feet (Scribner 32 ft) per acre	50,853

Pretreatment and Posttreatment Stand Statistics, by Treatment

Pretreatment and posttreatment stand statistics for all species combined are given in table 3-3, and table C-1 (appendix C). Note that these values are calculated from standing tree measurements on the permanent plots and will not be in complete agreement with values given in chapter 5 that are based on log scale and areas that include road right-of-ways.

Pretreatment and posttreatment diameter distributions are illustrated in figures 3-4 through 3-9. Visual appearance of the various treatments immediately after harvest is illustrated in figures 3-10 through 3-15.

Pretreatment and Posttreatment Regeneration Statistics, by Treatment

A pretreatment regeneration inventory in late winter 1997 produced the estimates of number of trees given in table 3-4. Values are based on one 4-milacre plot per main plot except in the control, which is based on the four 4-milacre plots per main plot measured in 1999.

Text continues on page 33

Table 3-3—Summaries for pretreatment (winter 1997), posttreatment (fall 1998), and approximate removals of trees 5.6 inches and larger[a]

	H40	Number	Basal area	QMD	CVTS	CV6	SV632	RD
	Feet	Trees per acre	Square feet per acre	Inches	Cubic feet per acre		Board feet per acre	
Clearcut—16 plots, 40.5 acres								
Pretreatment	143.8	114.1	226.9	19.1	11,240.6	10,808.3	52,451.0	51.7
Removed		114.1	226.9	19.1	11,240.6	10,808.3	52,451.0	
Posttreatment		0	0	0	0	0	0	0
Two-age—16 plots, 43.1 acres								
Pretreatment	143.3	117.5	240.8	19.4	11,961.4	11,528.6	55,494.5	54.6
Removed		101.9	194.5	18.7	9,575.5	9,203.3	43,932.0	
Posttreatment	142.7	15.6	6.3	23.3	2,385.9	2,325.3	11,562.5	9.5
Patch cut—26 plots, 71.8 acres								
Pretreatment (71.8 acres)	146.2	97.9	231.0	21.4	11,578	11,191	55,384	50.4
Removed[b] (71.8 acres)		45.4	70.9	16.9	3,560	3,392	16,245	
Thinned (54.8 acres)		29.1	21.2	11.9	1,073	973	4,103	
(Fraction of total)		(0.49)	(0.23)		(0.23)	(0.22)	(0.19)	17.0
Patches 17.0 acres		97.9	231.0	21.4	11,578	11,191	55,394	
(Fraction of total)		(0.51)	(0.77)		(0.77)	(0.78)	(0.81)	
Posttreatment (71.8 acres)	143.2	52.5	160.1	23.6	8,017	7,799	39,139	32.9
Thinned (54.8 acres)		68.8	209.8	23.6	10,504	10,218	51,281	43.2
Group selection—19 plots, 37.7 acres								
Pretreatment (37.7 acres)	146.3	101.6	239.0	20.8	11,919	11527	57,149	51.9
Removed[b] (37.7 acres)		59.0	104.8	18.0	5,037	4,814	23,243	
Thinned (30.1 acres)		48.2	70.9	16.4	3,299	3,119	14,682	
(Fraction of total)		(0.65)	(0.54)		(0.52)	(0.52)	(0.50)	
Groups (7.6 acres)		101.6	239.0	20.8	11,919	11,527	57,149	
(Fraction of total)		(0.35)	(0.46)		(0.48)	(0.48)	(0.50)	
Posttreatment (37.7 acres)	144.2	42.6	134.2	24.0	6,882	6,713	33,906	27.4
Thinned (30.1 acres)		53.4	168.1	24.0	8,620	8,408	42,467	34.3

Table 3-3—Summaries for pretreatment (winter 1997), posttreatment (fall 1998) and approximate removals of trees 5.6 inches and larger[a] (continued)

	H40	Number	Basal area	QMD	CVTS	CV6	SV632	RD
	Feet	Trees per acre	Square feet per acre	Inches	Cubic feet per acre		Board feet per acre	
Thinning—16 plots, 32.9 acres								
Pretreatment	143.5	129.1	254.9	19.0	12,624	12,161	54,846	58.2
Removed		57.8	62.5	14.1	2,821	2,658	7,746	
Posttreatment	145.7	71.3	192.4	22.3	9,803	9,536	47,100	40.7
Control—15 plots, 31.6 acres								
Posttreatment	155.1	112.0	261.2	20.7	13,577	13,106	65,792	57.2

[a] All values are expressed on a per acre basis, excluding area in roads and reserves. H40 = height of the 40 largest trees per acre, QMD = quadratic mean diameter, CVTS = total stem cubic foot volume, CV6 = merchantable cubic foot volume to a 6-inch top diameter inside bark, SV632 = Scribner board foot volume to a 6-inch top diameter inside bark in 32-foot logs, and RD = relative density (Curtis 1982). For patch and group treatments, only part of the treatment unit was clear felled, and the remainder was thinned.

[b] Removals are based on the difference between the pretreatment and posttreatment plot inventories. They included the cut and 1 year of growth. Total removals in the patch and group treatments are divided into removals by patches or groups, and removal as thinnings from the surrounding matrix. There were four patches with a total area of 17.0 acres and ranging from 2.15 to 6.98 acres. There were 16 groups with a total area of 7.6 acres and ranging from 0.05 to 1.32 acres.

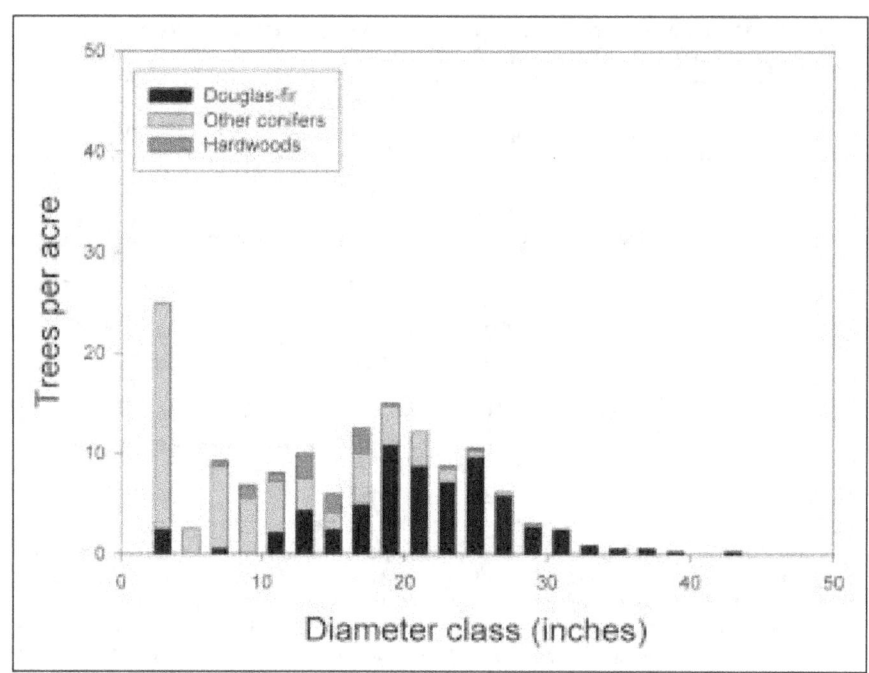

Figure 3-4—Diameter distribution of clearcut stand, pretreatment.

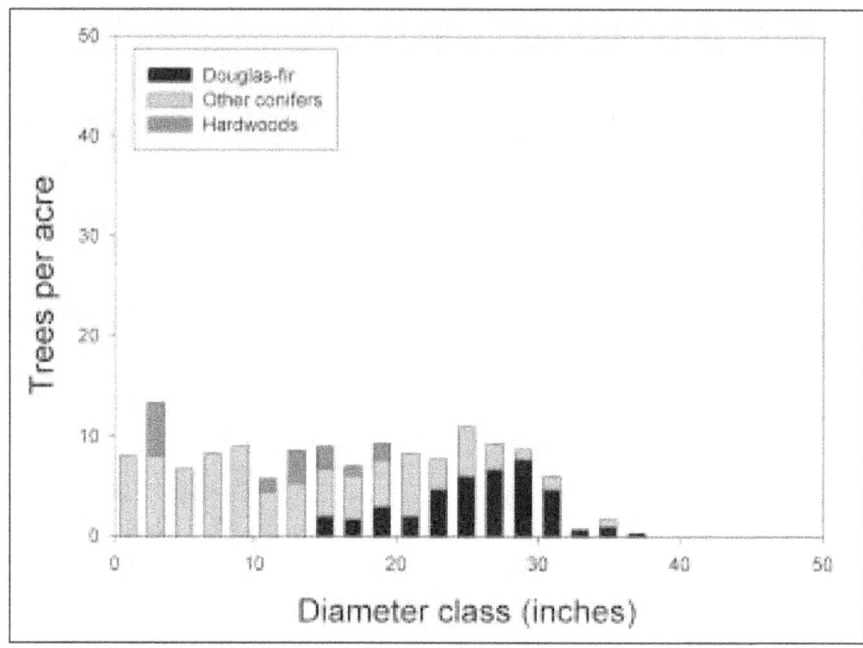

Figure 3-5—Diameter distribution of control (no treatment) stand.

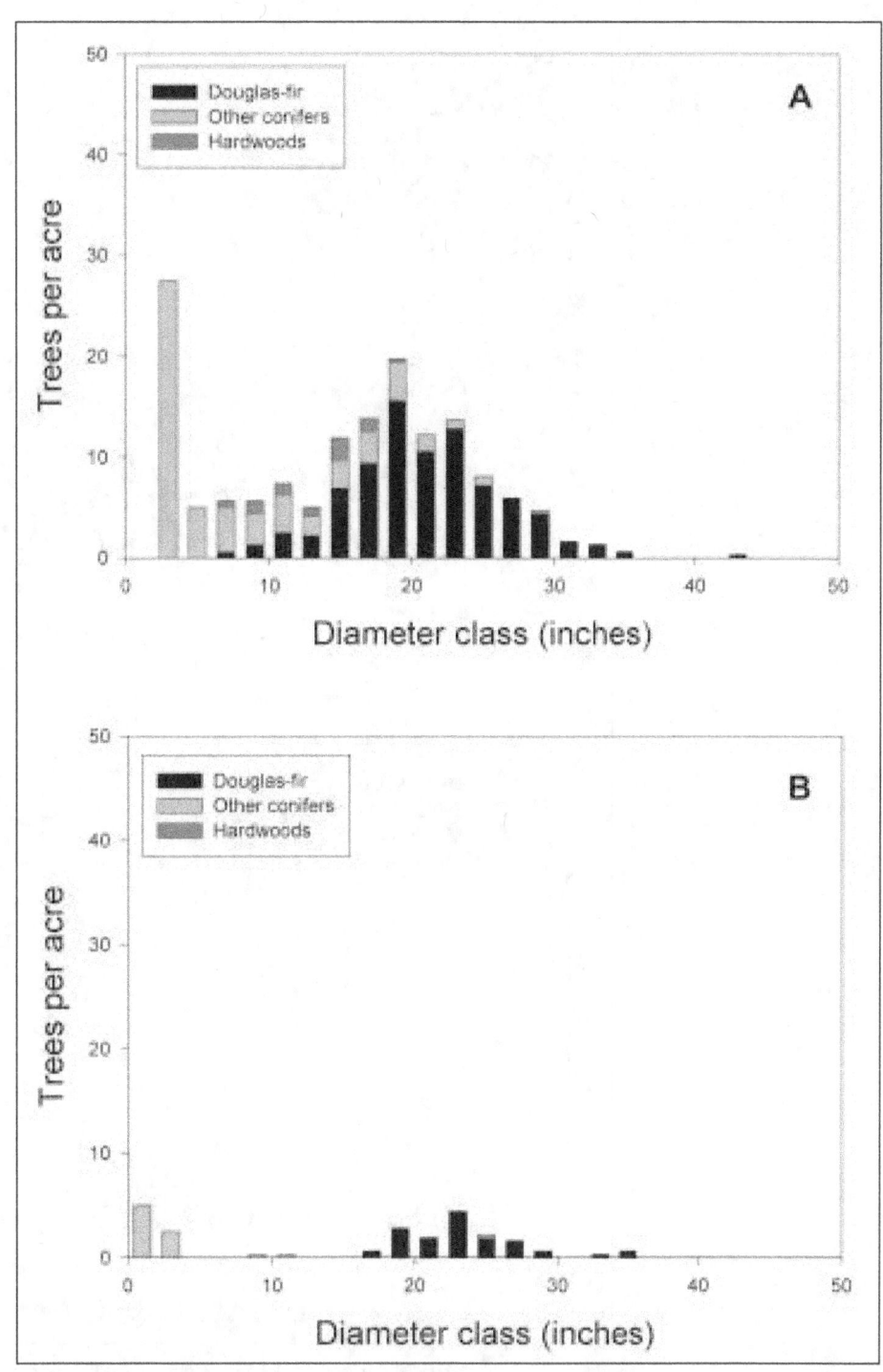

Figure 3-6—Diameter distribution of two-age treatment (a) before cut and (b) after cut.

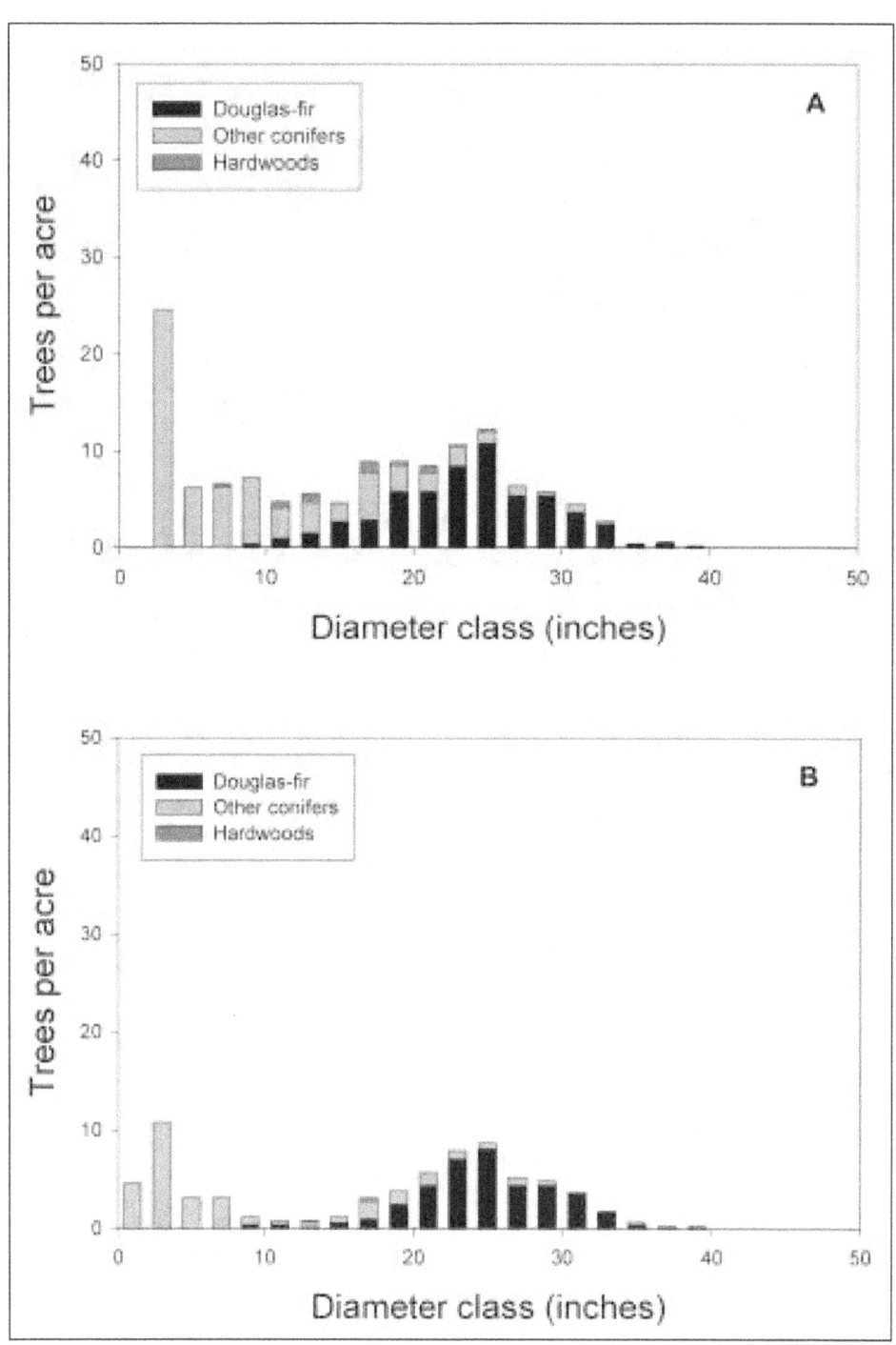

Figure 3-7—Diameter distribution of patch cut treatment (a) before cut and (b) after cut.

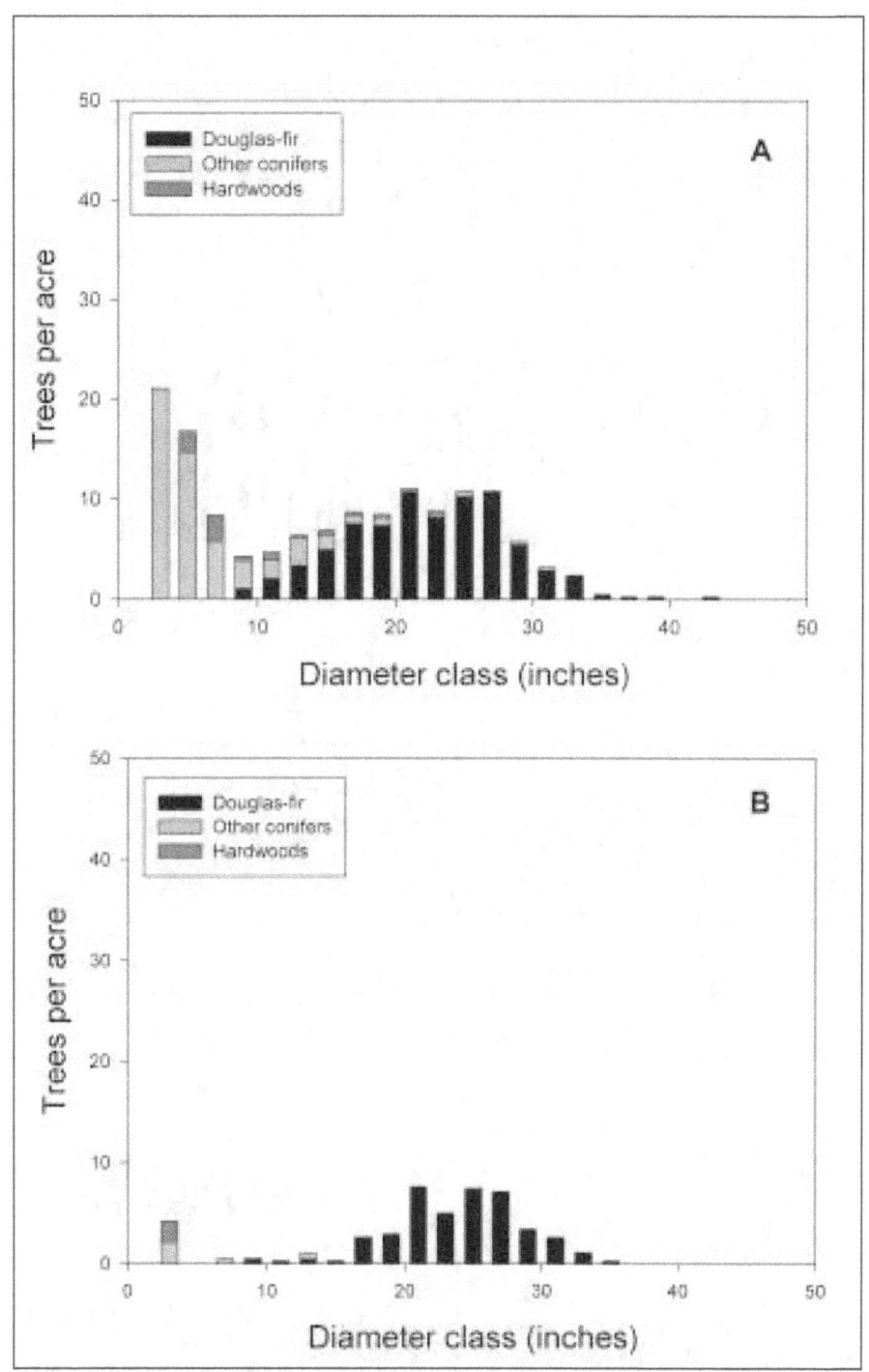

Figure 3-8—Diameter distribution of group selection treatment (a) before cut and (b) after cut.

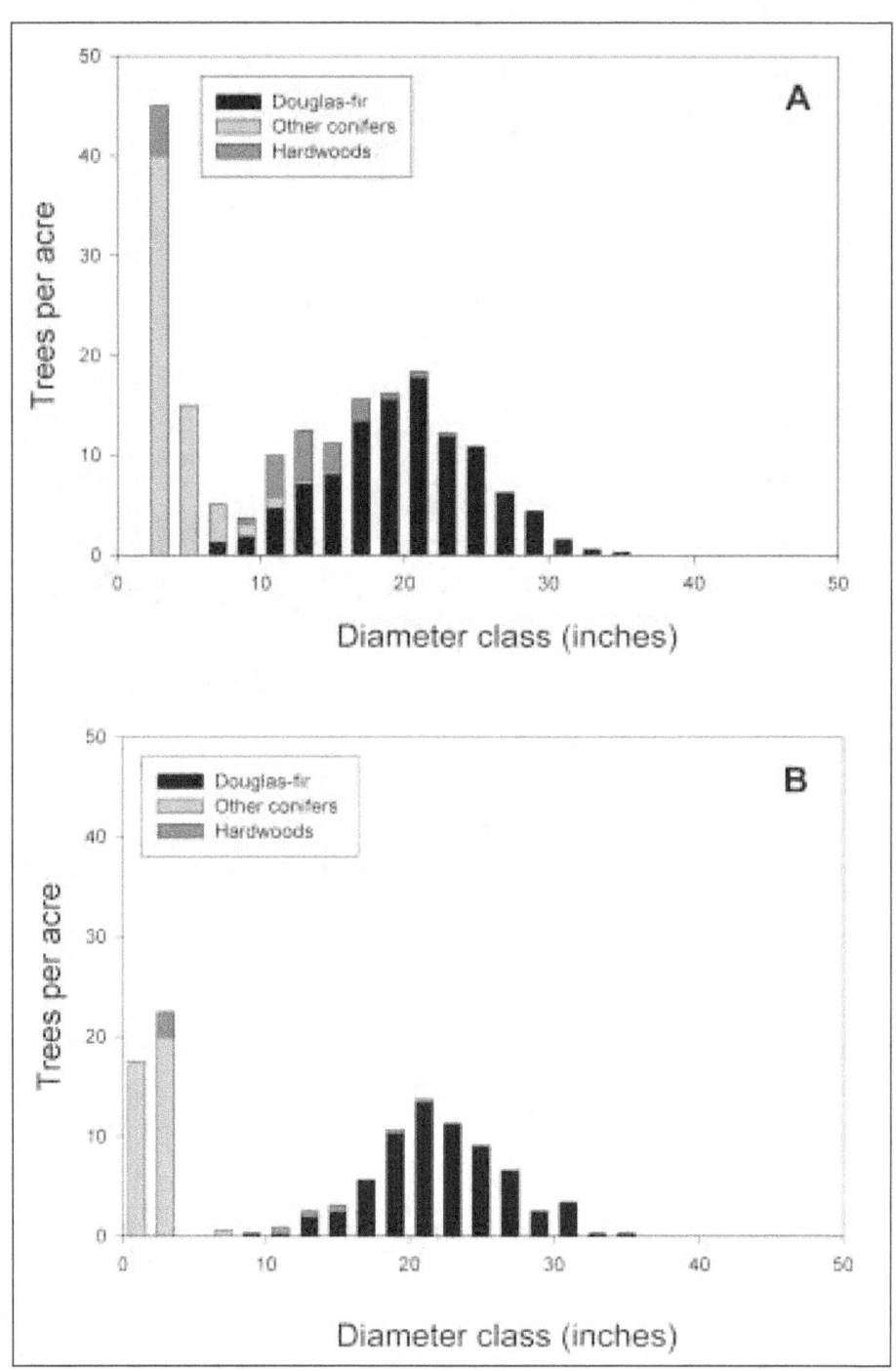

Figure 3-9—Diameter distribution of thinning treatment (a) before cut and (b) after cut.

Photo by Gordon Bradley

Photo by J. Alan Wagar

Figure 3-10—Clearcut unit immediately after harvest: (a) horizontal view and (b) aerial oblique.

A

Photo by Gordon Bradley

B

Figure 3-11—Two-age unit immediately after harvest: (a) within-stand view and (b) aerial oblique.

Photo by J. Alan Wagar

Photo by Gordon Bradley

Photo by J. Alan Wagar

Figure 3-12—Patch cut unit immediately after harvest: (a) within-stand view and (b) aerial oblique.

Photo by Gordon Bradley

Photo by J. Alan Wagar

Figure 3-13—Group selection unit immediately after harvest: (a) within-stand view and (b) aerial oblique.

Photo by David Marshall

Figure 3-14—Continued thinning unit immediately after harvest.

Figure 3-15—Control (untreated) unit.

Table 3-4—Pretreatment trees >1.0 foot tall and <1.6 inches diameter at breast height

Treatment	Number of 4-milacre subplots	Mean number of trees per subplot	Standard deviation of subplot values	Mean number of trees per acre[a]
Clearcut	16	8.19	14.2	2,047
Two-age	16	3.63	5.2	906
Patch cut	26	14.58	16.0	3,995
Group selection	19	2.26	5.1	566
Repeated thinning	16	2.53	2.9	656
Control	60	15.39	17.3	3,848
Overall mean				2,003

[a] Nearly all western hemlock.

Photo by Gordon Bradley

Virtually all advance regeneration was western hemlock. Given the small samples and high variability, there is little evidence of real differences among treatment units; any differences were slight and of no importance from the standpoint of the experiment.

Posttreatment measurements made in March and April 1999 of four 4-milacre subplots per main plot in all treatments (fig. 3-3) provided the estimates of natural regeneration in table 3-5. (Values for planted trees are omitted because these, nominally 400 per acre, were known to number about the same across all planted areas). Again, virtually all natural regeneration was western hemlock. Values for the patch cut unit have been further subdivided between matrix and patches. A similar subdivision is not feasible for group selection because of the small size of groups.

Although the above values are not directly comparable to the pretreatment values because of differences in sample size and arrangement, it is obvious that harvesting caused a substantial reduction in number of advance regeneration trees.

In the March 1999 inventory, all planted seedlings were identified by distance and direction from the subplot center stake, so that development of individual seedlings can be followed over time.

A second similar measurement made in spring 2000 (after the 1999 growing season) provided estimates of first-year mortality and growth of planted seedlings (tables 3-6 through 3-8) and extent of browsing damage. The overall mean was 29 percent of planted seedlings with recorded browsing damage. However, the small sample for the patch cut and group selection and some apparent inconsistencies in field procedure (inadequately specified criteria) preclude meaningful comparisons among harvest treatments.

Harvesting Damage to Residual Trees

In late 1998 and early 1999, each tree on the permanent plots was assessed for defect and damage. Codes included defects, such as forks, crooks, and dead tops, not related to harvesting operations. Damage caused by logging activities was also recorded, including live-branch breakage, root damage (usually caused by skidding), basal bark removal, and upper bole damage. A corresponding severity code also was recorded.

Stem defect occurrence was similar in all regimes where residual trees remained; all regimes had defects on fewer than 15 percent of the trees sampled (fig. 3-16). Frequency of damage from logging activities, however, was much higher in the two-age regime, being 68 percent of trees examined compared to 17 to 23 percent in the other treated stands.

In figure 3-17, logging damage is separated into four categories and corresponding severity levels, although the lowest severity level in each case is probably of slight practical importance for future development of the stands. Number of trees sampled in each treatment is indicated in the figure. Differences in frequency of damage were not great among treatments and damage was not severe, except in the case of the two-age stand.

The markedly greater frequency and severity of damage in the two-age regime reflects in part the much higher volume removed, compared to other partial cutting regimes. Also, the sample was much smaller on this regime than on the others (fig. 3-16). Frequency and severity of damage were also associated with season of harvest. The original plan was to begin harvesting in spring 1998 on the clearcut unit, and to do others subsequently. But a delay in road construction made it necessary to harvest the two-age unit first, in spring when the bark was slipping. This undoubtedly made the damage considerably more severe than would otherwise have been the case and is consistent with the high frequency of basal bark removal and upper bole damage.

Table 3-5—Natural regeneration immediately after treatment; number of trees >1.0 foot tall and <1.6 inches diameter at breast height, planted trees excluded

Treatment	No. of subplots	Mean number per subplot	Number per acre[a]
Clearcut	64	0.42	105
Two-age	64	.86	215
Patch, entire unit	104	3.88	970
In patches only	23[b]	1.47	368
Between patches	78[b]	4.67	1,168
Group selection	76	2.05	513
Repeated thinning	64	1.02	255
Control	60	15.39	3,848

[a] Nearly all western hemlock.
[b] Three subplots omitted because of overlap.

Table 3-6—Mean diameter growth at 6-inch height of measured planted Douglas-fir trees after one growing season

Treatment	Mean growth	Number of trees
	Inches	
Clearcut	0.18	100
Two-age	.16	81
Patch cut	.19	18
Group selection	.14	26

Table 3-7—Mean height growth of unbrowsed planted Douglas-fir trees, first growing season

Treatment	Mean height growth	Number of trees measured
	Feet	
Clearcut	0.26	34
Two-age	.35	56
Patch cut	.43	12
Group selection	.30	17

Table 3-8—Mortality of planted Douglas-fir trees, first growing season

Treatment	Number of trees on subplots	One-year mortality
		Percent
Clearcut	105	5
Two-age	93	9
Patch cut	21	14
Group selection	35	17
Weighted mean	—	9

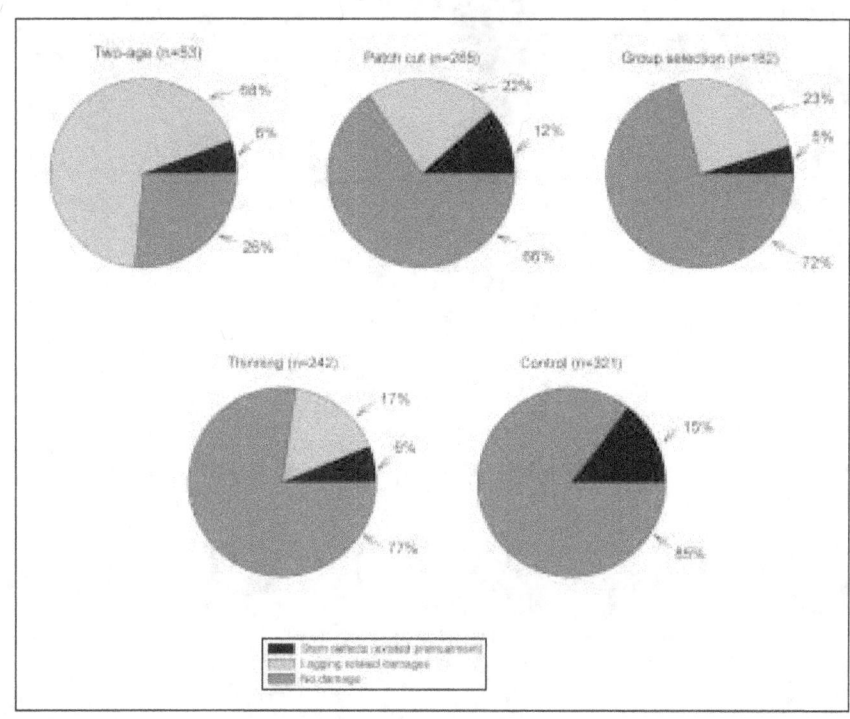

Figure 3-16—Frequencies of stem defects and logging-related damage, by treatment.

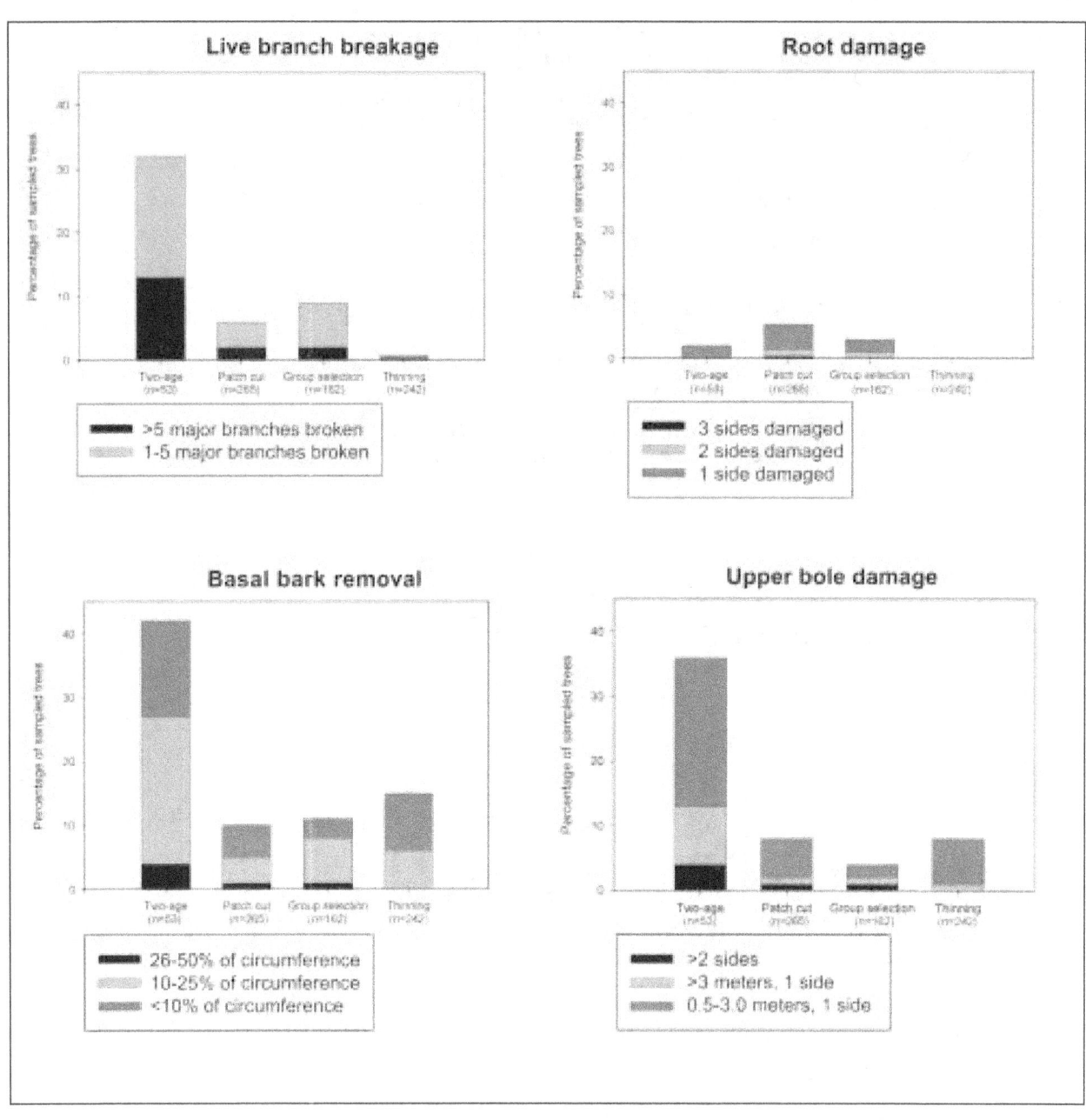

Figure 3-17—Damage to residual trees caused by logging activities, by category and severity. (Damage codes and severity ratings not recorded at significant levels were omitted.)

Windfall Losses

In September 2002, four winters after harvest, all trees that had blown down since harvest were located on unit maps, identified by species and direction of fall, and measured for diameter. If the tree was a Douglas-fir, it was examined for indications of root rot. These trees were nearly all uprooted rather than broken. Data were plotted on a map of the experimental area, and each wind-thrown tree was shown in relation to the regimes and patches and gaps that were created (fig. 3-18).

A total of 374 trees blew over during the period from logging in summer of 1998 until the September 2002 inventory (table 3-9). Windthrow was present in all units. About 90 percent of the windfall trees were in the patch cut, clearcut, and two-age units. Of this 90 percent, 44 percent were in the patch cut, 22 percent in the clearcut, and 34 percent in the two-age units. The other units accounted for about 10 percent of the windthrow. The trees that are listed for the clearcut were in the adjacent stand along the northern and eastern border of the unit and in the small reserve patches that were left on the unit. Windfalls in the patch cut and group selection units were mostly associated with the edge of a patch or group. The group selection unit was in a somewhat more topographically sheltered area than the patch cut. Most of the windthrow was western hemlock (72 percent). Douglas-fir was 25 percent, with the remainder being a few western redcedar and red alder. The large proportion of windfall in western hemlock is further emphasized by the fact that the posttreatment stands were (by number of trees) primarily Douglas-fir (75 to 98 percent) with the exception of the control, which was only 36 percent Douglas-fir. The western hemlock blown down in the two-age treatment came mostly from the reserve areas within the unit, as only a small proportion of western hemlock (3.8 percent of the trees) was left in the residual stand.

Quadratic mean diameters (QMDs) of the Douglas-fir and western hemlock (table 3-9) wind-thrown trees were similar to the pretreatment stand QMDs (app. table C-1), but tended to be smaller than the posttreatment QMDs, which were somewhat increased by the harvest of smaller trees. The QMDs of the other species (western redcedar and red alder) were smaller than that of Douglas-fir and western hemlock. Western hemlock has a shallower rooting system than Douglas-fir and would be expected to be less stable. In all treatments except the repeated thinning unit, over 60 percent of the Douglas-fir wind-thrown trees had indications of root rot. All Douglas-fir that blew over in the control had root rot present.

The closest weather station with records for this period is in Olympia, Washington, approximately 14 miles northeast of the study site and 1,000 feet lower in elevation. During the period October 1998 through September 2002, there were 170 occurrences of peak winds of 28 knots (32 mi/hr) or greater. These averaged 30.5 knots (35.1 mi/hr) and generally came from the south (average azimuth of 176 degrees), although they ranged from 150 to 260 degrees. The larger peak winds tended to come from the south to southeast. The greatest peak windspeed recorded was 42 knots (48 mi/hr) on January 29, 1999, and was from the south (table 3-10). The six greatest gusts were 38 knots (44 mi/hr) or greater, and all occurred from late November 1998 to early March 1999. This matches the observation that most of the windfall appears to have occurred within the first 2 years after the treatments were applied.

The direction of fall of wind-thrown trees was quite variable (fig. 3-18, table 3-11), and apparently was much influenced by local topography, cutting pattern, opening configuration, and presence of root rot, in addition to the overall direction of the highest speed winds.

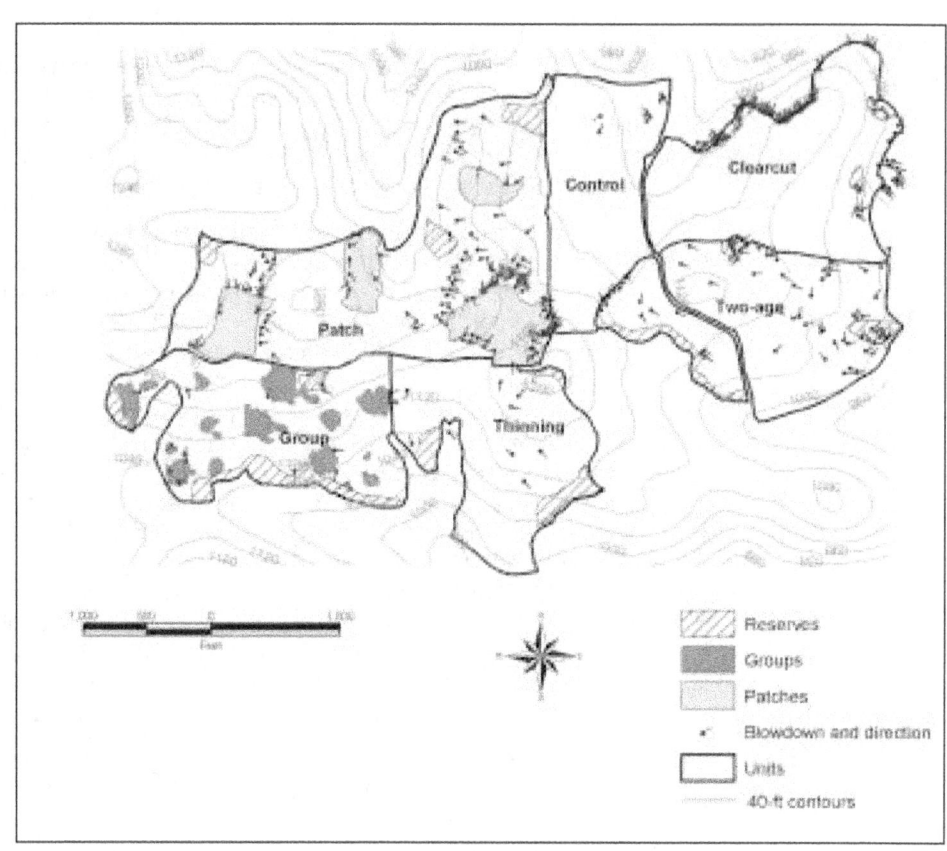

Figure 3-18—Location and direction of fall of trees wind thrown between October 1998 and September 2002. Shaded areas indicate the reserves.

Table 3-9—Wind-thrown trees at the Blue Ridge installation by treatment unit and species

Treatment	Total trees (trees per acre[a])	Species	Proportion of all windfalls by species	Proportion of Douglas-fir windfalls with root rot	Average (range) diameter at breast height
					Inches
Clearcut[b]	114	Douglas-fir	0.21	0.67	20.1 (6.1-33.6)
		Western hemlock	.74		12.7 (3.6-27.6)
		Other	.05		13.3 (10.0-16.6)
Two-age	75	Douglas-fir	.32	.63	19.5 (8.6-26.9)
	(1.60)	Western hemlock	.68		15.7 (5.4-27.0)
Patch	148	Douglas-fir	.17	.73	20.2 (4.3-31.9)
	(1.96)	Western hemlock	.82		15.9 (3.6-31.4)
		Other	.01		7.6
Group	20	Douglas-fir	.55	.73	19.2 (6.2-29.4)
	(0.46)	Western hemlock	.35		12.0 (5.6-22.3)
		Other	.00		7.8 (6.3-9.2)
Thin	9	Douglas-fir	.55	.20	19.2 (6.2-29.4)
	(0.25)	Western hemlock	.23		12.0 (5.6-9.2)
		Other	.22		7.8 (6.3-9.2)
Control	8	Douglas-fir	.63	1.00	19.4 (16.5-21.0)
	(0.25)	Western hemlock	.37		11.5 (6.8-18.0)

[a] Area including the reserve areas but not roads.
[b] Trees listed were in margin of adjacent stand or small reserved patches.

Table 3-10—Extreme windspeeds 1998-2002 as recorded at Olympia, Washington

Windspeed	Characteristics of the Beaufort wind scale	Number of records	Average direction (range)
Knots[a]			Degrees
28-33	Whole tree in motion and difficult to walk	149	177 (150-260)
34-40	Breaks twigs off trees and impedes progress	20	169 (150-200)
41-47	Slight structural damage occurs	1	180

[a] Knots x 1.1508 = miles per hour, knots x 1.852 = kilometers per hour.

Table 3-11—Wind-thrown trees, by treatment unit and direction of fall

Direction of fall	Clearcut	Two-age	Patch	Group	Thin	Control
			Number of trees			
N	38	18	28	4	1	1
NE	21	14	30	1	1	1
E	11	17	44	5	1	0
SE	16	12	24	3	2	1
S	1	0	7	3	3	1
SW	2	3	4	2	0	1
W	4	0	4	1	0	0
NW	21	11	7	1	1	3
Total	114	75	148	20	9	8

Brush Control

As of the end of 2002, the only vegetation control done was a small amount of spraying in September 2002 for brush control in that part of the two-age unit southwest of the road leading to the clearcut unit, two patches in the patch cut unit (one in the southeast corner, the other in the north central portion), and one small area at the old mill site in the western end of the group selection unit. Areas and costs as provided by DNR are summarized below. Agent and dosage used was 37 oz Accord + 15 oz Entry II in 10 gal water per acre.[3]

Unit	Area treated	Cost per acre	Total cost
	Acres	*– – – Dollars – – –*	
Two-age	12	85	1020
Patch cut	7	138	966
Group selection	1	95	95

Future Operations at Blue Ridge

Present planning assumes a 15-year entry cycle for harvest cuts and commercial thinning. Minor changes will remain possible until the time of the second entry. This does not imply that all areas will be thinned 15 years hence. Only that they will be inspected and thinning will be done on any portions of the area that are found to be in suitable condition at that time.

Timing and extent of any future precommercial thinning and brush control will be determined according to need.

Stand measurements and measurements of regeneration development and understory will be repeated at 5-year intervals, corresponding to one-third of the entry cycle.

The grid of permanent 1/5-acre plots may not provide an adequate basis for evaluating development of regeneration in the small openings and patches of the patch cut and group selection treatments. Therefore, consideration should be given at the 5-year remeasurement to establishing some transects within these that would allow a better evaluation of effects of competition from the residual stand.

References

Curtis, R.O. 1982. A simple index of stand density for Douglas-fir. Forest Science. 23: 92-94.

King, J.E. 1966. Site index curves for Douglas-fir in the Pacific Northwest. Weyerhaeuser For. Pap. 8. Centralia, WA: Weyerhaeuser Forestry Research Center. 49 p.

Henderson, J.A.; Peter, D.H.; Lesher, R.D.; Shaw, D.C. 1989. Forested plant associations of the Olympic National Forest. Ecol. Tech. Pap. R6-ECOL-TP-001-88. Portland, OR: U.S. Department of Agriculture, Forest Service, Pacific Northwest Region. 502 p.

Pringle, R.F. 1990. Soil survey of Thurston County, Washington. Olympia, WA: U.S. Department of Agriculture, Soil Conservation Service. 283 p.

---

[3] The use of trade or firm names is for the convenience of the reader and does not imply endorsement by the USDA Forest Service of any product or service.

Chapter 4: Timber Sale Layout, Marking, and Compliance Costs

Scott Robinson and Jeffrey D. DeBell

Introduction

When evaluating economic aspects of various silvicultural regimes, land managers must consider not only the timber production (volume and value) and logging costs, but also the financial and staff resources required to implement these regimes. Foresters of the Washington State Department of Natural Resources (DNR) prepared and administered the timber sale associated with implementation of the various silvicultural regimes discussed in chapter 2. In brief, the regimes consist of (1) a conventional clearcut; (2) retention of reserve trees to create a two-age stand; (3) small patch cuts dispersed within a thinned matrix, repeated at 15-year intervals to create a mosaic of age classes; (4) group selection within a thinned matrix on a 15-year cycle; (5) repeated thinning on an extended rotation; and (6) an untreated control. The regimes were applied on operational-size units of 30 to 70 acres each. The DNR kept detailed records of the staff time spent on sale layout, marking, and compliance for each of the regimes that received an initial harvest treatment (i.e., the first five), and collected information on the scaled volume of logs removed from each unit. This chapter describes the various activities performed by DNR foresters, including how activities varied among the regimes, and summarizes staff time as hours per acre and per volume removed to facilitate meaningful comparisons among the regimes. In addition, the implications of the findings and how such matters might change in future applications are discussed.

Timber Sale Layout, Marking, and Compliance Activities

The typical sequence of timber sale preparation activities for a conventional clearcut is (1) general reconnaissance; (2) road location and traverse; (3) location, marking, and traverse of the boundary; (4) marking of wildlife trees; and (5) cruising. For a typical thinning or other partial cut, the sequence would be about the same except that marking of wildlife trees may not be required and marking of cut or leave trees may be needed, depending on how the contract is structured. As road-building and timber harvest activities occur, staff time is needed to assure compliance with general and specific requirements related to the sale. These activities are described below.

General Reconnaissance

Location of an area suitable for the timber sale is the first step in sale preparation. This also involves stream identification, typing, and mapping. The need to locate a very uniform forest area, large enough to encompass six operational-size units, required much more time than is usual for location of a timber sale unit. This activity was done by both DNR and Pacific Northwest Research Station (PNW) staff, could not be allocated to individual regimes, and therefore is not included in our cost summaries.

Road Location and Traverse

Road location is determined primarily by topography and effective yarding distance of the equipment expected to operate on the site. It was not influenced by differences in silvicultural regimes tested in this study. One could argue that different cutting treatments require different equipment and therefore influence road location indirectly, but all regimes in this study were harvested with the same equipment. Any given section of road usually served more than one treatment, and it did not seem useful to try to divide those sections of road among units. We therefore did not allocate time spent on road location and traverse (or compliance during road building) among the silvicultural regimes; thus, this time is not reflected in our costs. Similarly, acreage and harvested timber volume associated with road rights-of-way were not included in calculations of costs per acre or per volume.

Location, Marking, and Traverse of Boundaries

We were able to divide time spent on boundary work among units, so this time is reflected in the data. We cannot, however, think of any reason that this should differ as a function of silvicultural regime. Any apparent differences most likely are due to chance differences in perimeter-to-area ratios between various regimes.

Marking of Wildlife Trees

Wildlife tree requirements under Washington forest practice rules were primarily written with clearcutting in mind, and therefore are more difficult to apply to regimes that maintain substantial amounts of overstory trees throughout a stand or management unit. For instance, requirements for a typical clearcut involve leaving about five trees per acre as wildlife trees. We did not think it made sense to simply apply this requirement within each opening created in the patch cut regime. Rather we designated wildlife trees throughout the entire stand unit when the first set of groups or patches were laid out; this approach seemed to be more responsible and conservative, and likely to provide more beneficial habitat over time.

Marking of Cut Trees

Trees to cut were marked in three regimes that involved thinning in the initial entry: (1) repeated thinning with extended rotation—residual stand to be in the range 160 to 180 ft^2/acre, except for designated reserve groups, with cutting primarily from below but with some larger trees removed as needed based on stem quality, vigor, and spacing; (2) patch cut; and (3) group selection. The matrix portions of the latter two regimes were marked throughout for thinning more or less as described above for the repeated thinning regime; this was done prior to location and marking of specific patches or groups. Prisms were used to monitor marking as it progressed.

Marking of Leave Trees

Trees were marked to leave in the two-age treatment, with a target of 15 trees per acre. Spacing was kept reasonably uniform by pacing a grid and marking a suitable tree nearest to each point.

Location of Skid Trails

A system of permanent skid trails was located throughout the patch cut treatment to allow all future patches to be reached without having to yard logs through regenerating patches. The skid trails were planned in much the same way that a road system would be planned, taking into account topography and yarding distances.

Location, Traverse, and Marking of Patches

Layout of patches involved several steps. First, the entire patch cut treatment area was divided into patches of different sizes, located so that each patch bordered a permanent skid trail. Then each patch was assigned a harvest date, so that harvest entries would be distributed throughout the entire area and would involve patches of all sizes. Finally, the patches to be cut in the first entry were marked. Although patches could have been marked with boundary tags, all trees to be cut within the patches were marked in the same color paint used in the thinned matrix surrounding it.

Location and Marking of Groups

Location and size of groups were determined according to procedures developed by the researchers. From each odd-numbered permanent plot (chapter 3), a group center was located at a random azimuth and distance (restricted to avoid overlap among groups). Size (area) of the group was selected randomly from a list of sizes ranging from two trees to 1.5 acres, and trees were marked for cutting from the center until the plot size was achieved.

Cruising

Costs associated with presale timber cruising were not kept. All units (excepting the control, which was not harvested) were measured by using variable plots. The number of sample points for each unit was determined by size of unit. For the patch and group selection treatments, the sampling grid was laid over the unit, and if the marked patches or groups were not adequately sampled, a different grid with additional plots was used. For this reason, one could expect a slightly higher cruising cost per acre for these two treatments.

Planning Meetings and Paperwork

All timber sales involve time spent in planning meetings with resource managers and on forms and other paperwork essential to the appraisal, actual sale, and harvest. This sale also required many additional meetings with research scientists because nearly every activity could affect or be affected by the objectives of the study. Such meetings accounted for the majority of total time (240 hours) spent on meetings and paperwork. The time could not be allocated to specific regimes, however, and is not included in the cost comparisons.

Compliance

Compliance entailed all aspects of administering the sale as it progressed. Cutting was monitored to assure that trees being cut were those designated for harvesting within the sale boundaries, and that soil and tree damage remained within acceptable limits. Because the sale was cut by a logging contractor and DNR sold specific log sorts to mills, compliance also involved checking to assure that trees were bucked to specifications of the log sorts and that all truckloads were appropriately scaled before leaving the sale area.

Cost Comparisons

Acreage, volume removed, and total staff time are listed for various sale activities for each unit (harvest treatment) in table 4-1. Also, staff time is shown per acre and per volume removed to allow more meaningful comparisons among the units or regimes. Data on time per unit volume removed were summarized graphically to illustrate trends among the harvest treatments (fig. 4-1).

Expressed as cost per acre, layout costs were lowest for the simplest, most uniform regime (e.g., clearcut) and highest for the most complex regime (group selection). Per acre costs for the repeated thinning regime were similar to those for the two-age and patch cut regimes. Although the thinning option was both simple and uniform, it had a substantially higher cost than the clearcut because individual trees were selected and marked for removal on all acres. Cost per unit of wood volume removed was inversely correlated with volume of wood removed. As a result, differentiation among the regimes

Table 4-1—Timber volume removed and hours spent on Blue Ridge sale by treatment unit and activity

	Clearcut	Two-age	Patch cut	Group selection	Thinning
Volume removed, (thousand board feet)[a]	1,986	1,591	1,264	595	323
Area, roads and reserves excluded (acres)	40.5	43.1	71.8	37.7	32.9
			Total hours		
Layout	32	26	44	33	28
Compliance	76	52	73	42	33
Marking	15	122	172	147	84
Total	123	200	289	222	45
			Hours per thousand board feet		
Layout	.016	.016	.035	.055	.087
Compliance	.038	.033	.058	.071	.102
Layout + compliance	.054	.049	.092	.126	.189
Marking	.008	.077	.136	.247	.260
Total	.062	.126	.229	.373	.449
			Hours per acre		
Layout	.79	.60	.61	.87	.85
Compliance	1.88	1.21	1.02	1.11	1.00
Layout + compliance	2.67	1.81	1.63	1.98	1.85
Marking	.37	2.83	2.40	3.90	2.55
Total	3.04	4.64	4.03	5.88	4.40

[a] Excludes 413 thousand board feet removed in road construction.

was greater when costs were expressed per unit volume than when costs were expressed per acre (table 4-1 and fig. 4-1). Costs per unit of volume removed for repeated thinning and group selection regimes were on average twice those associated with the patch cut regime, three times those for the two-age regime, and 6 to 7 times those for the clearcut. In many cases, managers will be more interested in cost per unit of volume removed than cost per acre, particularly when assessing returns from individual timber sales. Cost per acre may be useful for examining broader questions related to staffing needs and optimizing the mix of management systems on a landscape or ownership within constraints of budgets and staffing.

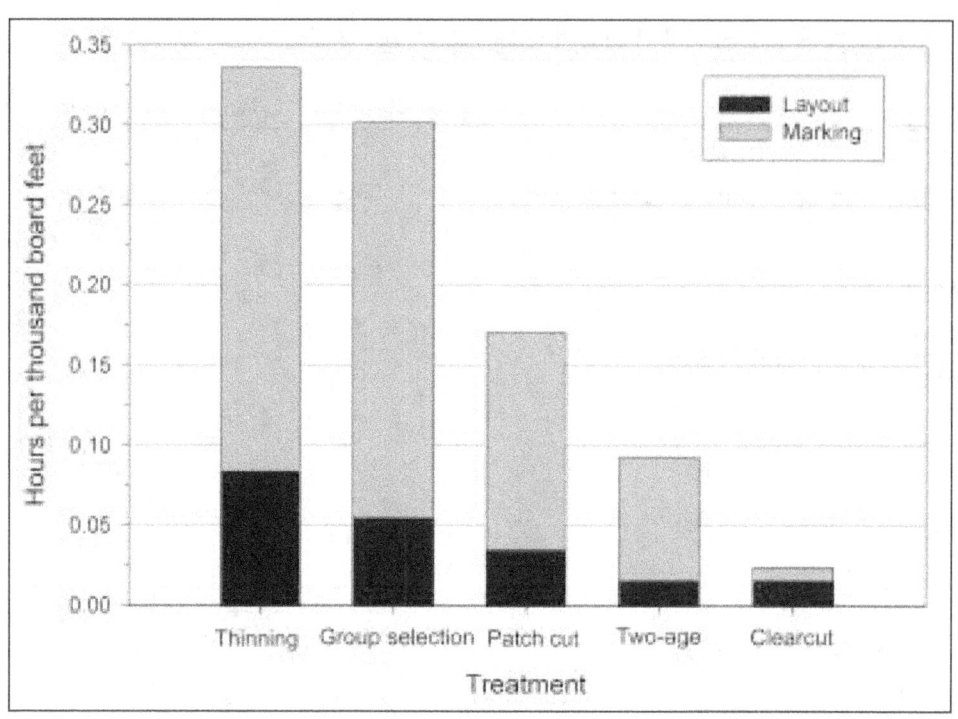

Figure 4-1—Sale layout and marking costs in hours per thousand board feet (Scribner), by treatment unit and activity.

Discussion

It is important to keep in mind that the costs for the group selection, patch cut, and two-age regimes would likely decrease somewhat if these treatments became common practice. There are always inefficiencies associated with trying new approaches, and these inefficiencies are reduced as experience with the system increases. Also, research projects normally take more time than routine operations because of the extra effort made to apply the treatment as closely as possible to the specifications of the experimental design. This "research effect" was probably greater for complex treatments than for simple, uniform treatments.

Two other factors affected the layout and administration costs: (1) the type of contract used for this sale and (2) the tree marking that was done. The DNR usually sells stumpage for a lump sum (normally used for clearcuts) or by weight scale (normally used for commercial thinnings in relatively young stands). For this project, however, a new approach was used where DNR contracted the logging and sold specific log sorts to several different mills (or buyers). As a result, log processing and sorting issues that usually are an issue for the purchaser became the business of the DNR contract administrator. This change in responsibility required extra time at the beginning of the sale while the contract administrator learned the new process and required greater effort throughout the sale. The two-age and clearcut regimes were the first units cut, so the contract administration (compliance) costs for those treatments were somewhat inflated compared to what would be required once the contract administrator was familiar with the process.

In this sale, trees were designated for retention or harvest in all treatments (except clearcutting, where only wildlife trees were marked) to help assure adherence to the intended specifications. Such marking, of either cut or leave trees, is not a routine part of forestry operations in western Washington (except for marking small numbers of leave trees for wildlife reasons during harvest operations). Therefore, the foresters doing the marking were less efficient than they would be if marking became common practice, as it is in eastern Washington. If these silvicultural treatments became commonplace, costs could be reduced in two ways. First, with more experience, the foresters would be able to mark much faster than was the case in this study. Second, the need for marking might be reduced or eliminated by specifying the desired result in the contract and letting the loggers choose the trees to cut. This latter approach is not without risk, however, and works best in young, uniform stands where differences in value among individual trees are not great. In older stands where individual tree values are large and variable, it can be more difficult to get the desired result. This is particularly true in mechanized harvesting operations, where the operator of the felling equipment may not have a clear view of stem defects higher in the tree stem. Moreover, if the purchaser is paying for the logs by weight, as is often the case in DNR thinning sales, there is strong incentive for high grading. Thus, reductions in marking costs are likely to be somewhat offset by the need for more detailed contract compliance work during felling operations.

An additional point to consider is timing of costs and returns of the newer or alternative regimes compared to customary regimes. Recall that the extremes of total cost per unit volume removed occurred in the clearcut and repeated thinning regimes, the two most common harvesting practices currently in use. Thus, costs for preparing and administering sales associated with the other systems fall within the range of those associated with routine operations. Furthermore, the higher cost of thinning occurs in midrotation and provides early cash returns, and the landowner still benefits from a lower harvesting cost at the end of the rotation when the stand is clearcut. With the group selection and patch cut regimes, all harvesting entries consist of a combination of thinning and complete harvest of small or large openings; costs are therefore incurred at an intermediate level, and cash returns are provided at more frequent intervals.

Effects on agency or corporate staff and budget also can be important considerations. Although differences in layout and compliance costs may at first appear insignificant compared to log values generated by this timber, an increase in costs that appears insignificant when compared to current sale values may still represent a substantial increase in annual staff personnel and costs. For organizations that must operate on a fixed percentage of sale value (DNR) or may have other staffing or budgetary constraints, such increases in cost may render some of the regimes infeasible, particularly when log markets are weak and stumpage prices decline.

Chapter 5: Harvesting Methods and Costs

Stephen E. Reutebuch and Leonard R. Johnson

This chapter describes the methods used to collect harvesting cost data and presents comparative harvesting costs for the initial harvest on the five units on which harvesting was done in 1998.

Silvicultural Regimes

The Capitol Forest study includes six silvicultural regimes as discussed in preceding chapters. The initial harvest treatment of five of the units (clearcut, two-age, patch cut, group selection, and repeated thinning) was conducted from April to September of 1998. There was no harvesting on the control.

Per-acre log volumes harvested from each of the units are given in table 5-1. These volumes are based on log scale on the entire unit including areas in roads and reserve groups and will therefore differ somewhat from volumes calculated from the permanent inventory plots, which are based on standing tree measurements and exclude roads and reserve areas.

Harvesting Methods and Equipment

All units were similar in soils, stand conditions, and topography. All units were harvested during the same year by a single contract logging crew using the same array of equipment.

All tree marking was done before harvesting operations began. A Timbco[1] 445-B feller-buncher was used to mechanically fell most trees up to 30 inches in diameter. Oversized trees were manually felled after the feller-buncher had cut an area.

Most skidding was completed with a D5H Caterpillar tractor fitted with a grapple. (A newer Model 527 tractor was used for the last few weeks of skidding). Whenever possible, trees were skidded as whole trees to the roadside. A Koehring 6644 hydraulic shovel, fitted with a grapple, was used to bunch for the tractor in the clearcut unit, two-age unit, and the large patches in the patch cut unit. A Caterpillar 320 hydraulic shovel,

---

[1] The use of commercial names is for the convenience of the reader and does not imply endorsement by the USDA Forest Service of any product or service.

Table 5-1—Volume harvested from each of the six units

Treatment	Net volume harvested
	Thousand board feet per acre,[a] Scribner
Clearcut	43.6
Two-age	3.8
Patch cut	15.6
Group selection	13.4
Thinning	8.6
Control	0

[a] Total area including roads and reserves.

fitted with a Waratah processing head, was used to delimb, buck, and deck logs at processing sites along roadside. The majority of the area was skidded downhill or across slope. A brief description of the harvest method used in each unit is given below. Coulter (1999) gives a more detailed analysis of the harvesting operations for each unit.

Clearcut Unit

All trees in the unit up to approximately a 30-in stump diameter were mechanically felled by the Timbco feller-buncher. The operator felled trees so that they were well aligned for extraction by the Caterpillar tractor. Owing to the large tree size, the feller-buncher operator did not attempt to bunch felled trees into convenient turns for the Caterpillar tractor. After the feller-buncher had completed its work, a faller then manually felled oversized trees.

The Koehring shovel, fitted with a grapple, was then used to build turns for the tractor. This turn-building operation entailed picking up felled trees and aligning their butts so that the tractor could easily back up and grab the turn with its grapple. The shovel operator would also buck a 40-ft log from the ends of trees that were too large for the tractor to skid as whole trees. In areas that were within about 150 ft of the road, the shovel would simply swing trees to the roadside for processing.

Once the tractor had picked up a turn, the operator would skid the load of trees to a roadside processing area and drop the load. The tractor would then drive the machine in reverse back to the shovel to pick up another turn. The tractor and the bunching shovel were not limited to designated skid trails; therefore, each machine traversed most of the unit.

At the roadside processing area, the Caterpillar 320 processor immediately delimbed and bucked the turns and stacked the logs along the roadside. Usually within hours, a Caterpillar 325 hydraulic log loader sorted and loaded the processed logs onto trucks at roadside. After the unit had been skidded, the loader moved through the area to pile slash. The feller-buncher, shovel, tractor, and loader all traveled through most of the unit. The processor stayed within about 50 ft of the roadside.

Two-Age Unit

The two-age unit was felled, bunched, skidded, processed, loaded, and slash was piled in approximately the same manner as the clearcut unit. More care had to be used to avoid damage to the residual stand. The Koehring shovel could not swing long pieces through a large arc because of the 50-ft spacing between residual trees. The residual trees also restricted the travel paths of equipment within the unit area.

The feller-buncher, shovel, tractor, and loader all traveled through most of the unit. The processor stayed within about 50 ft of the roadside.

Thinning Unit

The thinning unit was felled with the feller-buncher, except that oversized trees were manually felled. Once a tree was severed from the stump, the operator kept the tree in a vertical position. He then carried the tree to the nearest skidding corridor and laid the tree in the corridor with the butt end toward the direction of skidding. In some instances, when the tree was very large or the ground was steep, this careful positioning of the tree for skidding was not possible. Because the thinning was done from below (i.e., predominantly smaller trees were cut), the feller-buncher could effectively handle and bunch a larger percentage of the stems than in units with heavier cuts. The Koehring shovel was not used in the thinning unit because the residual stand spacing was too tight to allow it to operate without excessive stand damage. The tractor operator skidded predominantly along the corridors established by the feller-buncher, taking care to minimize damage to residual trees. The trees were processed into logs and loaded at roadside with the same processing and loading equipment as in the other units. Because only 8.3 thousand board feet (MBF) per acre were removed, the log loader only piled slash on or around the processing areas, not in the interior of the stand. Owing to the steepness of the topography, much of the unit was skidded sideslope to avoid pulling loads uphill. This resulted in longer skidding distances.

The feller-buncher and tractor traveled through most of the unit, with the tractor staying within thinning corridors. The processor and loader stayed within approximately 50 ft of the roadside.

Patch Cut Unit

The patch cut treatment consisted of removing trees from four large patches (1.6 to 5.2 acres each) composing approximately 20 percent of the area, combined with thinning of the intervening matrix. The patches were cut by the same techniques and equipment used in the clearcut unit. The only differences were that the patches were much smaller than the clearcut unit, and in two of the patches, the logs had to be skidded through the thinned portion of the unit to the roadside for processing. The remaining areas between the patches were harvested by the same methods as in the thinning unit.

The feller-buncher and tractor traveled through those sections of the unit that were only thinned, with the tractor staying within the thinning corridors. The feller-buncher, shovel, tractor, and loader all traveled through the patches that were clearcut. The processor stayed within about 50 ft of the roadside.

Group Selection Unit

The group selection treatment consisted of removals ranging from individual trees to openings of up to 1.5 acres, distributed throughout the unit. The openings were cut concurrently with the thinning of the rest of the unit. The small group openings were not large enough to accommodate the shovel, so the tractor bunched and skidded the trees unassisted. Skid distances had to be increased in much of the unit to avoid direct impact on a small stream.

The feller-buncher and tractor traveled through most of the unit, with the tractor staying within thinning corridors. The processor and loader stayed within approximately 50 ft of the roadside.

Sorting, Loading, and Hauling Operations

After logs were processed with the CAT320 processor, they were decked along the roadside. A CAT325 hydraulic loader was used to sort the logs into 12 different "log sorts." The same loader also loaded log trucks throughout the day. Additionally, the CAT325 loader was used to pile slash in the completed units whenever it was not busy sorting logs or loading trucks.

Log trucks (net weight limit of 25 to 26 tons) were used to transport the 12 log sorts to different processing mills.

Salvage Logging Operation

During the soil disturbance survey (chapter 6), a tracked log loader was conducting a salvage operation in the area. This operation consisted of the loader picking out pulp chunks from the slash piles and from along the roadside. The loader was not allowed to travel more than 200 ft from the road. This salvage operation was completed before the disturbance survey in the patch cut, group selection, and thinning units, but not in the clearcut or two-age units. Disturbance caused by this salvage operation was minor because the loader only traveled in areas near the roadside where disturbance was already very high.

Observed Stump-to-Roadside Costs

Coulter (1999) conducted extensive time and motion studies of the operations in all units except the two-age unit. Reutebuch et al. (1999) also collected equipment movement and production data throughout the harvesting operation by installing global positioning system (GPS) receivers and digital dataloggers on harvesting equipment. Based on these studies, observed machine and associated labor costs per MBF for processed logs at roadside were computed for each unit on the basis of scheduled machine hours (table 5-2).

Normalized Comparative Stump-to-Roadside Costs

In many situations, the observed cost differences between harvest units were not due to the silvicultural system, but to machinery capacities, skid distance, and a combination of machinery efficiencies as affected by delays. For comparison purposes, costs also were computed after normalizing those variables that were not directly related to the silvicultural treatment. Specifically, the average machine travel distances, terrain slope, and delays owing to maintenance and bottlenecks in the processing stream were normalized, whereas the other variables (e.g., piece size and pieces per turn) that were related to silvicultural treatment were not adjusted.

Two other factors related to machine usage were found to affect production and costs. First, it was found that the use of the shovel to bunch for the tractor (in the clearcut, two-age, and large patches in the patch cut unit) resulted in higher costs than when the shovel was not used. This was because the high hourly machine rate of the shovel was not offset by the increased production of the tractor.

Second, the processor did not have sufficient capacity to keep up with the production rate of the tractor and therefore caused serious delays (averaging about 30 percent of the total scheduled tractor time). Given the limitation in processor capacity, increased production from the tractor owing to shovel bunching could not be effectively used.

Table 5-3 lists comparative machine and associated labor costs per MBF (Scribner) by silvicultural treatment in which these variables have been normalized, the use of the shovel for bunching has been dropped, and the delays caused by insufficient processor capacity have been reduced from 30 to 10 percent of scheduled machine hours for the tractor. The processor costs have been increased to reflect the use of a larger machine that would be needed to achieve 10 percent wait-for-processor delays. These costs can be viewed as costs under equal and improved operating conditions for the silvicultural treatment options.

Table 5-2—Observed machine and associated labor costs for converting standing trees to processed logs at roadside

Machine	Clearcut	Two-age	Patch cut	Group selection	Thinning
	Dollars per thousand board feet, Scribner				
Feller-buncher	12.76	13.78[a]	12.93	25.76	21.28
Tractor	8.85	9.50[a]	19.42	21.90	21.04
Shovel	10.77	10.77[b]	1.46	—	—
Processor	9.59	9.59[b]	14.48	14.33	14.26
Total	41.97	43.64	48.30	61.99	56.58

— = not applicable.

[a] Estimated felling and skidding costs by using the production time data collected electronically.

[b] Shovel and processor costs are assumed the same as in the clearcut unit (Coulter 1999).

Table 5-3—Normalized machine and associated labor costs for converting standing trees to processed logs at roadside

Machine	Clearcut	Two-age	Patch cut	Group selection	Thinning
	Dollars per thousand board feet, Scribner				
Feller-buncher	16.44	21.66	26.10	25.87	24.43
Tractor	9.56	12.46	12.82	11.58	20.09
Shovel	—	—	—	—	—
Processor	13.44	13.44	15.29	15.29	15.75
Total stump-to-roadside	39.44	47.56	54.21	52.74	60.27
	Percent				
Increase above clearcut cost	0	21	37	34	53

— = not applicable.

Table 5-4—Estimated total log cost delivered to the mill with one-way truck haul distance assumed to be 50 miles

	Clearcut	Two-age	Patch cut	Group selection	Thinning
	Dollars per thousand board feet, Scribner				
Trees to logs at roadside	39.44	47.56	54.21	52.74	60.27
Sort, load, and piling costs	10.61	10.61	12.02	12.02	12.44
Road maintenance cost	1.26	1.26	1.26	1.26	1.26
Move-in-and-out cost	2.42	2.42	2.42	2.42	2.42
Night watchman	2.12	2.12	2.12	2.12	2.12
Fuel truck	.45	.45	.45	.45	.45
Maintenance truck	.76	.76	.76	.76	.76
Log-scaling cost	4.38	4.38	4.38	4.38	4.38
Office overhead (5 percent)	3.07	3.48	3.88	3.81	4.20
Profit (10 percent)	6.45	7.30	8.15	8.00	8.83
Total harvest cost	70.96	80.34	89.64	87.95	97.13
Trucking cost	38.36	38.36	38.36	38.36	38.36
Total harvest and haul cost	109.32	118.70	128.00	126.31	135.49

Estimated Harvesting, Loading, Hauling, Scaling, and Associated Costs

In addition to the stump-to-roadside cost, there were many other costs associated with the harvesting operation that were not correlated with treatment costs. These costs (table 5-4) were estimated to allow a more complete economic analysis of the overall returns from the alternative harvesting options over a long period (chapter 8).

Sorting, Loading, and Slash Piling Cost

After trees were skidded to roadside and processed into logs, a CAT325 hydraulic log loader was used to sort and load logs onto log trucks. The cost of the loader was $123.77 per hour. It was assumed that the loader worked 10-hr shifts and loaded the same volume per day as produced by the processor. In the remaining time, the loader sorted logs and piled slash. The estimated costs for loading, sorting, and slash piling are summarized in table 5-4.

Road Building and Maintenance Cost

Because this cost is dependent on factors not specific to each treatment, an average cost of $1.26 per MBF was used assuming an average haul distance of 50 miles (Forest Engineering Research Institute of Canada 1999).

Equipment Move-In-and-Out Cost

The cost to move the harvesting equipment in and out was assumed to be $16,000. Prorated over the total volume harvested, this results in a move-in-and-out cost of $2.42 per MBF.

Security

A night watchman was hired to protect equipment at night and over weekends. The cost per week was assumed to be $700 for 20 weeks. Prorated over the total volume harvested, this results in a security cost of $2.12 per MBF.

Fuel and Maintenance Trucks

The contractor needed fuel and maintenance trucks on site at all times. Assuming a cost of $30 and $50 per day, respectively, for the fuel and maintenance trucks, the prorated cost is $0.45 and $0.76 per MBF.

Log Scaling Cost

The DNR paid $29,000 to have all logs scaled on site, resulting in a cost of $4.38 per MBF.

Logging Contractor Administrative Overhead

Assuming an administrative overhead cost of 5 percent on all contractor costs results in a contractor administrative cost of $3.07 per MBF.

Logging Contractor Profit Margin

A profit margin of 10 percent was assumed.

Estimated Truck Hauling Cost

No studies of trucking costs were carried out during the actual operations. However, all trucks were scaled and weighed for the entire operation. The total gross log volume harvested was 6,616,700 MBF (Scribner), the total net volume (less defect) was 6,171,510 MBF, and the net weight was 37,601 tons. The net weight per gross MBF was 5.683 tons. Given an average log truck net load of 26 tons, the average truckload volume was 4.6 MBF. This average load volume was used to estimate a trucking cost of $0.77 per MBF per mi. An average one-way trucking distance of 50 mi was assumed, resulting in an estimated trucking cost of approximately $38.36 per MBF.

Cost Summary

The observed stump-to-roadside costs were lowest for the clearcut unit ($41.97 per MBF) and highest for the group selection unit ($61.99 per MBF). After normalizing variables that were unrelated to treatment (ground slope, skid distance) and optimizing the harvesting equipment mix (i.e., the processor capacity increased, 10-percent delays waiting for processor, and the shovel not used to bunch), the clearcut ($39.44 per MBF) still had the lowest cost. The two-age ($47.56) was about 21 percent higher, the patch cut ($54.21) was about 37 percent higher, the group-selection ($52.74) was about 34 percent higher, and the thinning ($60.27) was about 53 percent higher than the clearcut cost.

When all associated costs (loading, sorting, scaling, trucking, road maintenance, etc.) were estimated, the clearcut cost was lowest at $109.32 per MBF. The two-age ($118.70) was about 9 percent higher, the patch cut ($128.00) was about 17 percent higher, the group selection ($126.31) was about 16 percent higher, and the thinning ($135.49) was about 24 percent higher than the clearcut cost.

References

Coulter, K.M. 1999. The effects of silvicultural treatments on harvesting production and costs. Moscow, ID: University of Idaho. 113 p. M.S. thesis.

Forest Engineering Research Institute of Canada. 1999. Log transportation cost model. Field Note: Loading and Trucking-67. Vancouver, BC. 2 p.

Reutebuch, S.E.; Fridley, J.L.; Johnson, L.R. 1999. Integrating realtime forestry machine activity with GPS positional data. Pap. No. 99: 5037. 1999 ASAE annual international meeting. St. Joseph, MI: American Society of Agricultural Engineering. 18 p.

Chapter 6: Soil Disturbance on the Five Harvested Units[1]

John F. Klepac and Stephen E. Reutebuch

Introduction

Over the past decade, public concern in the Pacific Northwest about the visual and ecological effects of clearcut harvesting has increased. In response, natural resource managers are testing new silvicultural approaches to determine if various levels of harvest intensity can reduce both visual and ecological effects while maintaining economically viable harvesting operations. During this same time, mechanized harvesting systems have been introduced that can efficiently handle the large trees typically encountered in second-growth forests of the Pacific Northwest. There are many unanswered questions associated with using new mechanized equipment in these new silvicultural regimes. In this chapter, we examine the level of soil disturbance associated with such new approaches.

Soil disturbance is inevitable with any mechanized harvesting system. Clayton (1990) reports that tractor operations disturb an average of 30 percent of the activity area compared to 4 percent for helicopter, 9 percent for skyline, and 23 percent for ground cable systems. Logging activity causes soil to be displaced, compacted, scarred, or churned. Removing the organic layer and exposing the mineral soil can result in erosion and increased sedimentation in streams. Amounts of erosion and stream sedimentation following logging may vary directly with the degree of disturbance caused by timber removal (Dyrness 1965). The degree or severity of disturbance can be influenced by factors such as type of equipment, soil type, moisture content, slope, time of year, and skid trail orientation (Allen et al. 1999).

In addition to soil surface disturbance, there are concerns about the effect of soil compaction on site productivity. Compaction can reduce infiltration and aeration, and growth potential of seedlings can be significantly reduced, although this is not invariably the

[1] This is a condensation of material presented in Klepac, J.F.; Reutebuch, S.E.; Rummer, R.B. An assessment of soil disturbance from five harvesting intensities. Paper No. 99-5052 presented at the 1999 ASAE annual international meeting. Toronto, Ontario, Canada.

case. Froehlich (1977) reports growth reduction ranging from 5 to over 50 percent. Because compaction is highest in skid trails and landings, it is desirable to minimize the total area occupied by these areas.

Soil surface disturbance was evaluated on the five units harvested in 1998 under different silvicultural prescriptions in the Blue Ridge installation of the Capitol Forest study. A comparison of percentage of soil surface area in eight disturbance classes is presented. Percentage of area in primary and secondary skid trails and processing sites for each method is also reported.

Study Area and Stand Conditions

Topography of the site is gently rolling, with most of the area having a slope from 10 to 30 percent, although some short sections have slopes up to 50 percent. Elevation ranges from about 1,000 to 1,300 ft. The entire area is mapped as the Olympic soil series (Pringle 1990). The Olympic series consists of very deep, well-drained soils that occur on benches, hillsides, and broad ridgetops. These soils formed in residuum and colluvium derived dominantly from basalt. They are classified as silty clay loams, silt loams, and clay loams. The Washington Department of Natural Resources (DNR) forest soil management interpretation guidelines allow ground skidding on these soils if conditions are not excessively wet (table 6-1). The entire area was harvested without shutdowns from wet conditions; equipment was moved, however, to avoid particularly wet areas during periods of heavy rainfall.

The Olympic soil series has a medium erosion potential on slopes of 0 to 30 percent, the predominant slope class for the study area. Surface erosion can be significant, and extensive erosion can occasionally occur on skid trails if the soil surface is heavily disturbed. The series also has high puddling and compaction potentials. High puddling potential indicates that water puddling occurs during wet soil conditions after equipment traffic has destroyed soil structure by compression and shearing. This results in an impermeable surface that ponds water. Puddling results in loss of productivity because of restricted air and water movement in the soil. Compaction increases with additional passes of equipment and is sensitive to soil moisture conditions. When wet, the soil will not support equipment.

Harvest

All units were comparable in soils, stand conditions, and topography. All units were harvested in the same year by a single contract logging crew using the same array of ground-based equipment (see chapter 5).

Five of the six treatment units in the study were harvested between April and September of 1998.

Volumes removed from each unit are given in table 5-1 in chapter 5. Volumes are based on actual Scribner log scale, rather than plot estimates, and include volume removed from roads.

Soil Disturbance Survey Methods

Each of five treated units was intensively surveyed to determine the amount of surface soil disturbance by using the point transect method as specified by McMahon (1995). The survey was conducted in early November 1998, several months after harvest. Parallel transect lines were run across each unit at 66-ft spacing. Lines were oriented either north-south or east-west, depending on the direction of machine travel during harvest and the shape of the stand (fig. 6-1). Along each transect line at regular distances of either 25 or 33 ft (larger units were sampled at 33-ft spacing along the transects), soil disturbance was visually assessed and assigned a disturbance classification. Points landing on primary or secondary skid trails or processing or deck areas were noted by assigning a code. These codes were later used to determine percentage of area of each of these

Table 6-1—Forest soil management interpretations for Olympic clay loam

Category	Rating
Slope stability	
Natural	Stable
Disturbed	Stable
Timber harvest	
Logging system limitation	Moderate
Compaction potential (moist)	High
Displacement potential (dry to moist)	Low
Puddling potential (wet)	High
Erosion potential	Medium
Regeneration	
Drought potential	Low
Plant competition	Severe
Windthrow potential	Low

Source: Washington DNR, n.d.

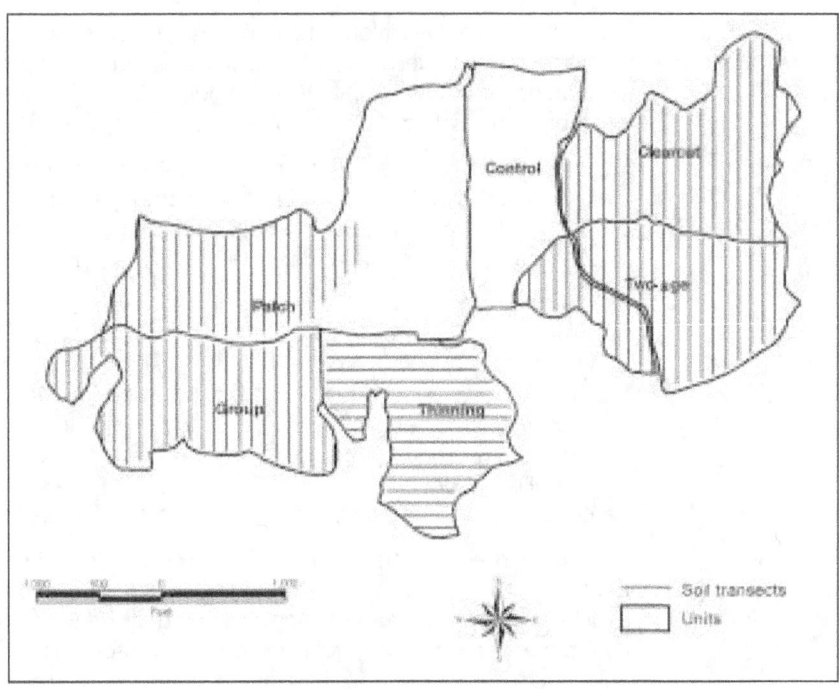

Figure 6-1—Surveyed harvest units and orientation of soil disturbance transect lines.

types of locations. Skid trails were defined as primary if they led to landings and secondary if they were branches of primary trails. The clearcut, two-age, commercial thinning, and group selection units were completely surveyed. Only the western half of the patch cut unit was surveyed owing to the large size of the unit. In the patch cut unit, points falling inside the clearcut patches were noted with a code so that they could be distinguished from those in the thinned portions of the unit. The control unit was not surveyed. Approximately 800 points were assessed in each surveyed unit. The disturbance classes were defined as follows:

1. Undisturbed—no evidence of machine or log movement over the point.

2. Disturbed with litter in place—litter was still in place with evidence of machine movement over the point. Typically this class had machine track marks.

3. Soil exposed and litter removed—bare soil visible. Disturbance could be from machine or log movements.

4. Litter and soil mixed—soil and litter layers were mixed together by machine or log movements.

5. Soil exposed with rutting over 4 inches deep—points where machine travel had created significant ruts.

6. Nonsoil—standing trees, stumps, logs, rocks.

7. Missing—point covered by slash or debris piles.

8. Newly deposited litter—points that had been completely covered during the logging operation with fresh needles, leaves, and fine branches, totally obscuring underlying litter and soil conditions.

Results

Percentage of observations in each disturbance class were calculated for each silvicultural treatment (tables 6-2 and 6-3). Because each sample point represents the same amount of area within a unit, the point percentages provide a direct estimate of the percentage of area of each disturbance class within a unit.

Percentage of Area in Each Disturbance Class by Silvicultural Treatment

Because this is only a single replicate of several planned future replications of the study, we cannot test significance of differences among treatments. Results are presented in terms of unit means. These unit means are based on large samples within each unit, and differences in means among treatments are consistent with logical expectations.

Considering the four classes in which the soil surface showed evidence of machine traffic or log movement (disturbed with litter in place, soil exposed and litter removed, litter and soil mixed, and soil exposed with rutting over 4 inches deep), the overall patch cut unit had the largest percentage of area disturbed with 50.6 percent. The small clearcut patches within the patch cut unit showed even higher disturbance at 61.0 percent. The clearcut and two-age units were nearly the same with 48.3 and 48.1 percent, respectively. Falling about midway among the treatments was the group selection unit with 41.0 percent. The thinning unit had the least amount in these four classes with 37.0 percent.

Combining the three disturbance classes containing some form of exposed soil (soil exposed and litter removed, litter and soil mixed, and soil exposed with rutting over 4 inches deep), the clearcut and patch cut units were nearly the same with 32.2 and 31.6 percent, respectively, followed by the two-age unit with 27.2 percent. The group selection and thinning units had the least amount of area in these categories with 23.8 and 22.5 percent, respectively. The small clearcut patches within the patch cut unit again showed even higher disturbance at 40.8 percent.

Table 6-2—Percentage of each unit containing each soil disturbance class

Disturbance class	Clearcut	Two-age	Patch cut Overall	Patch cut Thin	Patch cut Patches	Group selection	Thinning
			Percentage of unit				
Undisturbed	11.1	10.7	29.2	37.4	7.3	35.3	36.4
Litter in place	16.1	20.9	19.0	18.6	20.2	17.2	14.5
Soil exposed	16.5	11.8	12.7	11.5	15.9	11.2	12.1
Litter-soil mix	14.4	14.9	17.8	15.6	23.6	11.6	9.5
Exposed >4-in ruts	1.3	.5	1.1	1.0	1.3	1.0	.9
Nonsoil	7.0	10.1	5.3	4.4	7.7	7.1	5.5
Missing or slash	7.2	6.6	2.9	2.1	5.2	3.8	3.9
New litter	26.4	24.5	12.0	9.4	18.9	12.8	17.2
			Number				
Observations	769	785	850	617	233	885	775

Table 6-3—Percentage of each unit containing each disturbance class with nonsoil and missing or slash classes excluded

Disturbance class	Clearcut	Two-age	Patch cut	Group selection	Thinning
			Percentage of unit		
Undisturbed	12.9	12.8	31.8	39.6	40.2
Litter in place	18.8	25.1	20.8	19.3	16.0
Soil exposed	19.2	14.2	13.8	12.6	13.4
Litter-soil mix	16.8	17.9	19.4	13.1	10.5
Exposed >4-in	1.5	.6	1.2	1.1	1.0
New litter	30.8	29.4	13.1	14.3	18.9
			Number		
Observations	660	654	780	788	702

For those classes where a litter layer existed after harvest (undisturbed, disturbed with litter in place, and newly deposited litter), the thinning unit contained the largest amount of area with 68.1 percent, followed by the group selection and patch cut units with 65.3 and 60.2 percent, respectively. The two-age and clearcut units had the least amount of area with an existing litter layer with 56.1 and 53.6 percent, respectively. The small clearcut patches within the patch cut unit again showed even higher disturbance with only 46.4 percent of the area containing an existing litter layer.

Percentage of Area in Skid Trails and Processing Areas

In addition to determining percentage of area disturbed in each treatment unit by disturbance class, the percentage of area occupied by primary and secondary skid trails, processing areas, and log decks was also of interest (table 6-4). Total area in primary and secondary skid trails ranged from 16.6 percent (patch cut unit) to 21.7 percent (thinning unit). These results are comparable to those obtained by Stokes et al. (1995) for group selection and clearcut harvest methods using manual felling and articulated rubber-tired skidders. Their results indicate that total area in skid trails averaged 14.6 percent for group selection units and 22.4 percent for clearcut units. Total processing and deck area was similar for all units, ranging from 4.5 to 6.5 percent. The total area that was heavily traveled (i.e., trails, processing and deck areas) was very similar for all units ranging from 21.1 percent in the patch cut unit to 28.2 percent in the thinning unit.

Discussion of Soil Effects

Selection of the harvesting equipment and operating methods was not dictated by research needs. The equipment and methods selected were the result of standard timber sale practices of the DNR. Soil disturbance could be considerably different if a different array of equipment had been used and operated in a different fashion. For instance, if cable chokers had been used, rather than a grapple, the tractor might have been able to avoid traveling over much of the area. If the hydraulic shovel had not been used to bunch for the tractor, disturbance might have been lower in the clearcut, two-age, and patches in the patch cut unit. Use of designated skid trails in all units would have concentrated disturbance in the skid trails. Unfortunately, it was not possible to specify the equipment mix and operating methods for this study.

In general, as removal intensity increased, the percentage of undisturbed area decreased. The thinning unit had the highest percentage of undisturbed area, whereas the two-age and clearcut units were similar with the least amount. The clearcut, two-age, and small clearcut patches in the patch cut unit all had high volumes of timber removed. To accomplish this, machines passed over the units more times. More slash was generated, requiring piling by the loader, and in some areas, redistribution over the area by the tractor. Because the clearcut and two-age units had the most slash on the ground after harvest, these units had the highest percentages of area in the missing class.

The summary revealed that the two-age unit had the highest percentage of area "disturbed with litter in place." This is most likely a result of the machine operators' efforts to avoid damage to residual trees. Although most of the trees were felled, bunched, and skidded, care was taken to not hit or scrape the residual standing trees with either logs or equipment. This required the machine operators to concentrate their traffic more in the area between residual trees, only traveling near residual trees once or twice to pick up logs near them. This concentration of machine travel also is reflected in the higher percentage of area in skid trails (20.9) in the two-age unit, even though there were no designated skid trails.

Table 6-4—Percentage of each treatment unit within each location category

Location	Clearcut	Two-age	Patch cut	Group selection	Thinning
	Percentage of unit				
Primary trail	10.9	11.6	10.0	9.6	12.3
Secondary trail	8.5	9.3	6.6	8.4	9.4
Total trails	19.4	20.9	16.6	18.0	21.7
Process and deck area	6.3	5.5	4.5	6.0	6.5
	Number				
Observations	769	785	850	885	775

There was a general trend of increasing area of "soil exposed and litter removed" as removal intensity increased. The clearcut unit and small clearcut patches in the patch cut unit are similar with the highest percentage for this disturbance class. The two-age unit had a low percentage for this class and was similar to the group selection and commercial thinning. This is a result of more area being lightly traveled to avoid tree damage instead of being repeatedly traversed with associated loss of the litter layer.

Percentage of area with "litter and soil mixed" also was highest on the units with the highest removal intensities. The clearcut and two-age units were similar in the amount of area for this class. Surprisingly, the patch cut unit had the highest percentage of "litter and soil mixed," both in the portions that were only thinned and in the small clearcut patches. One possible explanation for this may be related to the feller-buncher operator's abilities. In about half of the area sampled in the patch cut, a new feller-buncher operator was being trained. This new operator was much less adept at positioning the machine and bunching trees in corridors. As a result, there may have been more impacts resulting from both increased feller-buncher travel and from poor positioning of trees for extraction.

In general, the percentage of area in "newly deposited litter" (fine needles and branches from limbs and tops) increased as removal intensity increased. The clearcut unit had the highest percentage for this class, followed by the two-age unit.

The amount of area containing ruts greater than 4 inches with soil exposed was low and similar in magnitude across all units. This result is a combination of two factors: soil displacement potential and use of wide tracks. The overall harvested area has a low displacement potential from timber harvesting activities. This soil characteristic, along with the use of wide-tracked harvesting equipment, resulted in little rutting.

Soil compaction is a major concern among land managers because it can reduce tree growth. Although soil bulk density was not measured in this study, past experience has shown that areas with the highest amount of compaction are usually primary skid trails and processing and deck areas. Percentage of area in skid trails and decks is not a direct measure of soil compaction; however, it is an indication of heavy equipment traffic usually associated with higher levels of compaction. In this study, total percentage of area in these high traffic classes was not correlated with volume of timber removed. Despite removal of much more volume per acre from the clearcut and two-age units, the skid trail assessment revealed that all units were fairly similar in the percentage of total area in skid trails and decks.

Percentage of area in these classes was probably influenced not only by the harvest method but also by the unit topography. The skid trail assessment revealed that the thinning unit had the highest percentage of area in skid trails. This unit had a very steep area at its north end. This feature prohibited the tractor from skidding trees located in the northern portion of the unit directly to the top of the unit. Instead, the tractor was required to skid trees across the unit along a gentler route. This resulted in long skid trails within the unit, and consequently more skid trails per unit area. It should be noted that assignment of harvest treatment to unit was random and not based on equipment constraints. Therefore, skid trail occurrence and frequency would most likely have been lower if the thinning unit had occurred in an area with gentler terrain. The thinning harvest method (i.e., bunching to corridors), however, concentrated travel within corridors by creating de facto skid trails.

Results from this study characterize soil disturbance resulting from one harvest entry into the units. No attempt was made to consider the possible links between soil disturbance and compaction, change in tree growth, sedimentation, or other processes. The silvicultural study plan specifies that the group selection and patch cut units, and possibly the thinning unit, will be treated again before the clearcut and two-age units are commercially thinned for the first time. Depending on the recovery rate of the soil, these multiple entries into the units could have a cumulative impact on soil compaction, particularly if machine traffic is repeatedly concentrated in the same corridors.

References

Allen, M.M.; Taratoot, M.; Adams, P.W. 1999. Soil compaction and disturbance from skyline and mechanized partial cuttings for multiple resource objectives in western and northeastern Oregon, U.S.A. In: Sessions, J.; Chung, W., eds. Proceedings of the International mountain logging 10th Pacific Northwest skyline symposium. Corvallis, OR: Department of Forest Engineering, Oregon State University: 107-117.

Clayton, J.L. 1990. Soil disturbance resulting from skidding logs on granitic soils in central Idaho. Res. Pap. INT-RP-436. Ogden, UT: U.S. Department of Agriculture, Forest Service, Intermountain Research Station. 8 p.

Dyrness, C.T. 1965. Soil surface condition following tractor and high-lead logging in the Oregon Cascades. Journal of Forestry. 63: 272-275.

Froehlich, H.A. 1997. Soil compaction: Why the controversy? Loggers Handbook. 37: 20-22.

McMahon, S. 1995. Accuracy of two ground survey methods for assessing site disturbance. Journal of Forest Engineering. 6(2): 27-33.

Pringle, R.F. 1990. Soil survey of Thurston County, Washington. Olympia, WA: U.S. Department of Agriculture, Soil Conservation Service. 283 p.

Stokes, B.J.; Kluender, R.A.; Klepac, J.F.; Lortz, D.A. 1995. Harvesting impacts as a function of removal intensity. In: Forest operations and environmental protection: Proceedings of a symposium. Tampere, Finland: IUFRO Project Group P3.11.00: 207-216.

Washington Department of Natural Resources [DNR]. [N.d.]. State soil survey, report for the Central Area. Unpublished report. On file with: Forest Land Management Division, Department of Natural Resources, P.O. Box 47001, Olympia, WA 98504-7001.

Chapter 7: Public Reactions Research

Gordon A. Bradley, Anne R. Kearney, and J. Alan Wagar

Introduction

The Washington State Department of Natural Resources (DNR) and the USDA Forest Service Pacific Northwest Research Station (PNW), in cooperation with the University of Washington College of Forest Resources, are conducting a joint study of the silvicultural, economic, and visual effects of alternative timber harvest patterns at Capitol State Forest near Olympia, Washington. This multidisciplinary effort provides a unique opportunity to examine tradeoffs among conflicting objectives and to explore concepts and opportunities for reducing such conflicts.

Within the total multidisciplinary effort, the specific study outlined here will explore how various visual cues affect public responses to alternative timber harvesting patterns as well as how personal knowledge and assumptions affect the interpretation of those cues. We will develop preliminary conceptual models explaining how selected segments of the public perceive alternative patterns of timber harvesting in the predominantly Douglas-fir (*Pseudotsuga menziesii* (Mirb.) Franco) Capitol State Forest. For the long term, it will be important to understand how people's perceptions of harvesting are affected by the information they have. Information levels seem likely to be especially important for evaluating harvest patterns that purposely include debris, snags, and other provisions for soil stability, wildlife habitat, and similar values.

To obtain as much information as possible at a reasonable cost, color photographs of sites will be used to survey people's reactions to alternative forest harvest patterns and the visual and cognitive cues within them. Photos have been found suitable for comparing the visual attractiveness or suitability of landscapes (Brown and Daniel 1984, Kaplan and Kaplan 1989). They also offer the advantage of cost effectiveness. This study will capture foreground, middle, and background views.

The initial phase of the study focused on foreground views at the Blue Ridge Study area. Middle and background views will be obtained on subsequent research plots on the Copper Ridge and Rusty Ridge study areas.

Visual Resources Literature

Several bodies of literature treat the subject of visual resources management, or forest aesthetics. These include (1) articles reporting on research studies, (2) agency manuals, and (3) professional guides. Research studies have approached the subject of visual resource management by identifying those "environmental attributes that are salient to scenic beauty" (Kaplan et al.1989). In most cases, slides or photographs of scenes are used to determine an individual's preference for a particular setting. These approaches differ in terms of what they attempt to measure within the landscape. There have generally been four domains of inquiry including physical attributes, land cover types, informational variables, and perception-based variables. The physical attributes approach focuses on the identification of physical attributes that affect preference, such as vegetation, sky, and water (Zube et al. 1975). The land cover approach focuses on traditional land cover types such as residential, industrial, forest, or agriculture as factors for determining landscape preference. The information approach focuses on individuals' understanding of landscapes and the extent to which a person would choose to explore the landscape in greater detail; factors that have emerged from this approach include coherence, complexity, legibility, and mystery as determinants in human preference for landscape scenes (Kaplan and Kaplan 1989). The important aspect of the information approach is the hypothesis that preferences will be greater with greater comprehension or understanding of what is going on in a scene. This is not to be confused with providing information about the scenes to test the influence that added information may have on preference ratings. Finally, perception-based studies simply ask respondents to view scenes and rate them according to how much they like the scene (British Columbia Ministry of Forests 1994). Mean preference values can be compared among scenes and, by using clustering techniques, one can begin to see patterns in the types of scenes that people prefer (Kaplan 1985, Kaplan and Kaplan 1989). It is this latter approach that the visual research on the Capitol Forest has taken.

In the context of forest aesthetics, visual preference research studies show that generally people share a similar view of what makes for an aesthetically pleasing landscape and which modifications create negative visual impacts. Overall, people tend to prefer landscapes that retain more standing green trees and that minimize the amount of residual material such as stumps and brush. Many studies have found that a sense of order is preferred in the landscape as indicated by high ratings for parklike settings, large trees, and landscapes that appear "natural." Also, ground cover and a mix of vegetation are generally preferred over bare soil and a uniform stand of trees (Bacon 1995; British Columbia Ministry of Forests 1981, 1994; Brown and Daniel 1984; Ribe 1989; Ulrich 1986). The time since initial harvest also is an important factor in determining visual preference. Over time, preference ratings improve for sites that have been intensively managed, and the differences among sites experiencing various silvicultural treatments diminish (Shelby et al. 2003). Although for much of the population preferences for forest scenes rise and fall in a similar pattern, preferences for certain scenes may differ based on a person's relation with the landscape. For example, a forest scene that has been significantly modified by a timber harvest might be rated higher by a person working in forestry than by a person who does not work in forestry.

The findings of empirical research have been incorporated into numerous texts, manuals, and guides that are used by various natural resource management agencies and professional organizations (Bradley 1996, Forestry Authority 1994, Lucas 1991, Northeast Regional Agricultural Engineering Service 1993, USDA Forest Service 1974, 1980).

The contribution that this study will make to the visual resource management literature is twofold. First it combines visual preference data with economic, biological, and physical data to establish the tradeoffs that are made in selecting a visually preferred harvest approach. This type of integrated study involving visual resources management has not been done before. Second, the precise silvicultural prescriptions for scenes that are used in forest preference studies typically are not well established. In this study, all attributes of the forest stands are known so that it is possible to report with some certainty the nature of the stand conditions with their associated preference ratings.

Preliminary Research

In order to develop the general approach and methods to be used in this research, a preliminary study was completed. Because this study of public reactions began well before harvests were completed on the study area, photographs (35mm slides) of similar harvest patterns from other areas were collected. Photos from existing files were much less useful than we had hoped, with most of them taken for other purposes at angles and scales that did not very well represent the visual effects of harvesting. We therefore made several trips to photograph stands at Capitol Forest, the College of Forest Resource's Pack Forest (near Eatonville, Washington), and elsewhere, augmenting the collection borrowed from files.

From this augmented collection, we selected slides representing the planned harvest treatments and as free as possible from such extraneous elements as prominent debris, misshapen trees, or unusual lighting. To check on our judgments, we asked senior silvicultural scientists and mensurationists with the PNW Research Station in Olympia and a staff forester with the Washington DNR to identify the treatment represented by each slide and tell how well it represented such treatment. We are comfortable that the selected slides represented the study treatments reasonably well. The main variables not controlled in these proxy slides are the amount of time since harvest, the time of year, and the amount of "greening up" that had occurred.

Because suitability for wildlife would seem to be an important consideration in people's ratings of timber harvest acceptability, we also asked University of Washington College of Forest Resources wildlife faculty to rate each slide for habitat quality. Their immediate response was, "Habitat for what? Different creatures have different requirements." Generally, however, they told us that habitat quality increases with (1) the amount of shrubs and ground cover present to provide food and shelter for wildlife (with areas having mostly bare ground being the least desirable) and (2) structural diversity (as when a multilayered canopy is created).

Developing and Testing a Survey Form

A survey form with a 5-point rating scale was developed. As part of its development, the form was tested on undergraduate students in an impact assessment class at the University of Washington. The purpose of this test was to make sure that respondents understood the approach to the study and found the response form to be functional.

Preliminary Preference Tests

After developing and testing the survey form, we scheduled data collection sessions with the Lewis County Farm Foresters, the Olympia Chapter of the Mountaineers, and DNR personnel at a meeting that included field personnel from the Olympia area and staff from the Commissioner of Public Lands office. Although selected somewhat opportunistically, these groups represent people likely to have quite contrasting attitudes toward timber harvesting. Following the survey, the authors provided a brief discussion of forest aesthetics research.

For the Farm Foresters and Mountaineers, the format was to provide a program for their evening meetings. At the beginning of the program, those attending were provided survey forms, shown slides of alternative harvest patterns, and asked to rate their level of preference for each scene by using the 5-point rating scale. Following the survey, the authors gave an illustrated talk on aesthetic treatments of forested landscapes, including an overview of research in this area.

Results and Preliminary Distribution

A comparison of preference ratings, by group (fig. 7-1), shows that although there is a substantial amount of overlap in how the groups respond to harvest techniques, there are areas of differences as well. In general, these differences were most pronounced between the Mountaineers and the other two groups (DNR and Farm Foresters). Tests done on student groups showed that students' preference ratings were very similar to the Mountaineers' ratings. These data suggest that forestry experts may view scenes differently as a result of their experience.

All three groups gave high preference ratings to control scenes that were "natural" in appearance, showing little human intervention. Likewise, there was little difference in the groups' ratings of scenes showing a very high degree of manipulation, such as a clearcut: the groups uniformly gave these types of scenes low ratings.

Where differences were found, they typically were for scenes where harvesting was evident but trees remained. Depending on the background and stance of the viewer, these scenes may have been viewed as good implementations of harvesting technique or as overly manipulated landscapes. For instance, a scene depicting a group selection harvest along with a significant amount of woody debris was rated low by the Mountaineers and moderately high by the other two groups. Likewise, a scene that showed new growth in a patch cut marked by straight harvest lines also was rated low by the Mountaineers and moderately high by the other two groups.

These results caution forestry professionals against assuming that others will react to harvest practices the same way that they do. Results of the preliminary preference tests have been shared through presentations to the DNR, other forestry professionals, and the academic community.

Blue Ridge Study

Work on the Blue Ridge study began prior to the actual harvest of trees. Prior to harvesting, a complete set of onsite photographs was taken in July of 1997 from plot center markers on all plots established by the PNW Research Station, Olympia. After the harvesting of the research plots, an additional set of photographs was taken from the same points on July 23 and October 1, 1998. During spring of each subsequent year through 2002, photographs were taken from the same plot markers.

Photos have been taken each year at the same time to control for seasonal and weather variation in the landscape. Photographs have been taken on sunny days in spring, after deciduous trees have leafed out. Taking the photos in the spring minimizes the factors that may influence preference ratings such as light angle, fall color, snow, or bare trees. Also, when taking photos, an attempt was made to capture the essence of the scene. Care was taken to include the elements of the landscape that were characteristic of a treatment, without showcasing them in a way that would unnecessarily influence a response. For example, where stumps were characteristic of the clearcut treatment, they were not displayed prominently in the center of a scene.

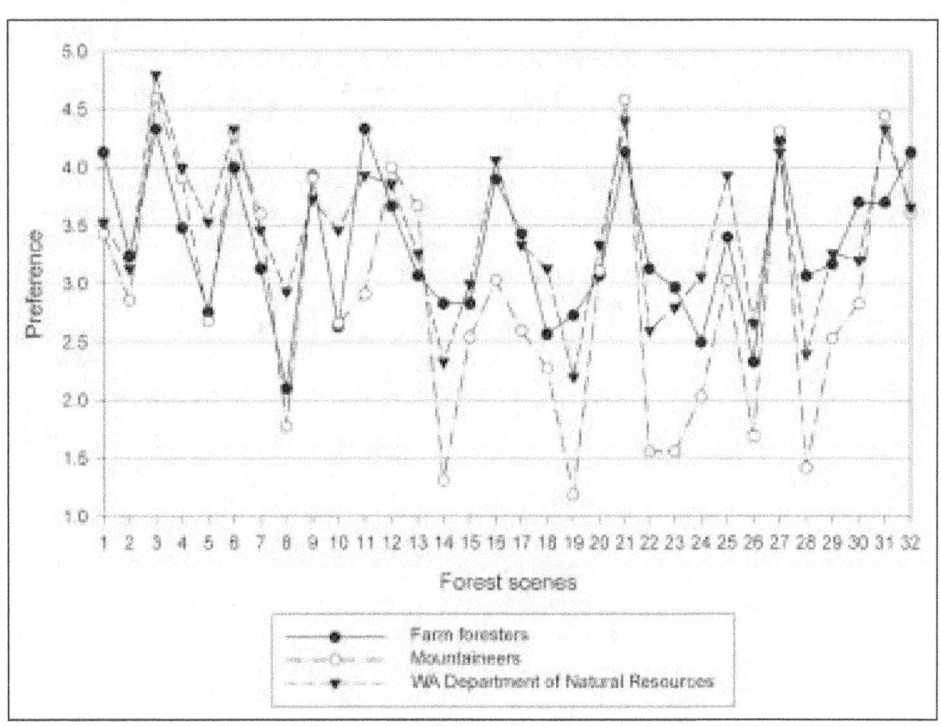

Figure 7-1—Preference ratings, by population group.

Survey Development

The preliminary preference study for this project obtained responses from subjects by showing slides, but it became apparent that this approach was limited in reaching the number of individuals and diversity of groups needed for the study. Therefore, a black-and-white photo questionnaire was developed that included scenes representing each of the treatment plots. To determine if the questionnaire achieved the same results as slide viewing, a class of approximately 100 University of Washington undergraduate students was divided in half with one group viewing slides, and the other group using the photo questionnaire. Responses from the two methods were almost identical for each of the scenes. Where there were slight variations in response, it appeared that the detail visible in the color slides accounted for the difference. Consequently, it was decided to use color photographs in the photo questionnaire.

The color photo survey was further tested on a graduate urban ecology class at the University of Washington. Explicit concern was for the ordering of the photos relative to other questions in the survey and for the clarity of instructions. Minor modifications were made to the survey. The survey was then printed in an 8.5- by 11-inch format, with an explanatory letter indicating the purpose of the research and assuring confidentiality for subjects if they responded to the survey. The survey was printed with a postage-paid imprint and return address on the back cover, so that when the survey was completed it could be easily returned to the University of Washington.

The survey contained 31 color photographs depicting the six treatment plots in the study. For each plot, approximately five photos representing different views of the treatment and varying amounts of greenup (i.e., time since harvest) were selected for inclusion in the survey. The photos were randomly selected for order in the survey. For each photo, respondents were asked to indicate how much they liked each scene. A scale of 1 = not at all, 3 = somewhat, and 5 = very much was used for the preference rating. The last 10 photos, which also represented scenes from each of the plots, requested additional information regarding why the respondents rated the scene the way they did. Finally, two additional scenes were included to show the appearance of the area surrounding the primary harvest pattern. Because there were some questions about how people might respond to the patch and group selection treatments when they were shown without the surrounding thinned forest, a scene was developed that showed the forest opening of the patch and group selection harvests with the denser forest on each side. The intention was to illustrate the general condition of the surrounding forest, or context in which the treatments were situated. For these two context scenes, a preference rating was requested along with the rationale for the response.

Beyond the photo portion of the survey, there were four pages of questions regarding knowledge and attitudes about various aspects of forest management, confidence in different forest management organizations to manage forests, and finally, demographic information including current residence, where the respondent grew up, and his or her affiliations with natural resource or environmental organizations.

Survey Administration

Selected groups of people were asked to participate in the study. Those funding the research and the researchers themselves were interested in how responses might differ among various groups of people. These groups included the general public (including both rural and urban residents), foresters, recreationists, environmentalists, and educators. Those sampled in the educator category were identified from a mailing list provided by the Office of the Superintendent of Public Instruction in Olympia, Washington. Foresters were sampled from a western Washington Society of American Foresters chapter. Environmentalists were represented by the Sierra Club. Recreationists included individuals from the Issaquah Alps Trails Club and other recreation groups who regularly use Capitol Forest. The Capitol Forest recreation group names were provided by the DNR. Finally, the general public consisted of individuals from both rural and urban addresses in western Washington. Approximately 750 individuals were sent surveys, and 210 responded (about 28 percent). Of those who responded, 32 were urban residents, 18 were rural residents, 55 were foresters, 51 were recreationists, 33 were environmentalists, and 16 were educators (population group for 5 respondents could not be determined). Although the above categories are not mutually exclusive, the authors stratified the samples by using mailing lists specific to each group.

Analysis of Survey

Several statistical procedures were used to analyze the data. Average preference ratings for the scenes in each treatment group (clearcut, patch cut, group selection, two-age, thin, and control) were computed. To determine if, indeed, the respondents discriminated among the various treatments in their preference ratings, a factor analysis was completed as well. Means then were calculated for the new groupings of photos that emerged from the factor analysis.

Differences among the six population groups on both treatment-based preferences and factor-based preferences were computed through two separate multivariate analyses of variance (MANOVAS), one for the six treatments and one for the four preference factors. The MANOVAs were chosen rather than separate univariate ANOVA tests for each dependent variable because of significant correlations among the dependent variables in each set. To determine which groups differ across which treatments and preference factors, Tukey HSD post hoc tests were conducted. (If the assumption of equal group variances, as tested by Levene's Test, was not met, then Dunnett's C post hoc tests were conducted and are so indicated in the tables.) The above procedures are discussed in SPSS 1999 and Green et al. 1997.

Preliminary Findings

Preference for Treatment Types

Significant differences in preference for the six treatment types were found among the six population groups ($F = 4.52$; $df = 30,770$; $p \leq 0.001$). Results are shown in table 7-1.

In general, foresters tended to show significantly greater preference than most other groups for treatments where tree removal left moderate to large openings (i.e., clearcuts, patch cut, and group selection); the difference was most striking for the clearcut treatment. Most groups tended to show moderate preference for the two-age treatment, with the exception of the environmentalists, who showed lower preference. All groups showed high preference for the commercial thin and for the control (although preference means were significantly lower for foresters than for the environmentalists and educators).

Factor Analysis Results

A principal components factor analysis with varimax rotation was run by using a factor selection criterion of eigenvalues greater than or equal to 1. The cutoff value for loading of individual scenes on a particular factor was 0.50. Scenes that loaded on more than one factor were eliminated.

Results of the factor analysis (table 7-2) show that, in general, respondents did not discriminate among the scenes based on treatment type. Rather, respondents tended to perceptually group scenes according to similar overall patterns of openings, tree size variation, and color (i.e., amount of green).

Preferences for Photo Factors

The MANOVA results show significant differences in the four preference factors based on population group ($F = 4.41$; $df = 20,472$; $p \leq 0.001$). Results are shown in table 7-3 and are depicted graphically in figure 7-2.

First, note (fig. 7-2) that all groups' preferences for the scene types follow the same trend, with "green natural appearance" being the most preferred, followed by "small greened-up clearings," "partial retention," and finally "large and or recent clearings."

Where differences existed, foresters and environmentalists tended to be at the two extremes with the other groups more or less in the middle. Foresters showed significantly higher preference for "large and or recent clearings" than did all other groups. Environmentalists showed significantly lower preference for "partial retention" than did foresters. Most of the groups' preference ratings in this category were moderately low to moderate. Environmentalists also showed significantly lower preference for "small or greened-up clearings" than did the urban public, foresters, and recreationists. All groups showed high preference for "green natural appearance."

Table 7-1—Preference* (and standard deviation) for treatment type, by population group

	Urban (n=32)	Rural (n=18)	Forester (n=55)	Recreation (n=51)	Environment (n=33)	Educators (n=16)
Preference for clearcut[†]	1.61a (.90)	2.04 (1.44)	3.08 a b c d (1.23)	1.51b (.74)	1.24c (.40)	1.28 d (.23)
Preference for two-age[†]	2.76 (.94)	2.73 (.95)	3.25a (1.22)	2.92b (.87)	2.23 a b (.60)	2.59 (.65)
Preference for patch cut	2.77 a f (.76)	2.75b (1.06)	3.46 a b c d e (.84)	2.65c (.81)	2.16d f (.54)	2.43e (.69)
Preference for group selection[†]	2.93 a e (.69)	3.00 (.95)	3.54 a b c d (.82)	2.89b f (.76)	2.47c e f (.51)	2.66d (.63)
Preference for repeated thin	4.06 (.60)	4.11 (.95)	4.06 (.62)	4.06 (.65)	3.83 (.50)	4.13 (.73)
Preference for control	4.42 (.81)	4.33 (1.00)	4.02 a b (.92)	4.44 (.66)	4.62a (.41)	4.73b (.48)

Note: Means sharing the same letter are significantly different at p ≤ 0.05.

* Mean preferences, on a 5-point scale with 5 = highest preference, are shown with standard deviations in parentheses.

[†] Dunnet's C post hoc test run.

Table 7-2—Results of factor analysis on treatment scenes

Scene types (factors) and descriptions	Overall mean	Standard deviation	Alpha[a]
Green/"natural" appearance This category included three control scenes, three commercial thin scenes (from 1999 and 2000, all showing greenup) and one group selection scene (from 2000 showing considerable greenup).	4.27	0.69	0.86
Small, greened-up clearings This category included two commercial thin scenes (from 1998 and 2000), two group-selection scenes (from 1999 and 2000) and two patch-cuts (from 2000).	3.33	.79	.84
Partial retention This category included five two-age treatment scenes (from 1998, 1999, and 2000).	2.85	1.00	.92
Large or recent clearings This category included four scenes of clearcuts (from 1998, 1999, and 2000 showing various degrees of greenup), a 1998 patch-cut, and a 1998 group-selection scene (both of these scenes were recently harvested).	2.12	1.12	.96

[a] Cronbach's coefficient alpha, a measure of scale reliability (on a 1.0 scale).

Table 7-3—Preference* (and standard deviation) for scene types, by population group

	Urban (n=25)	Rural (n=13)	Forester (n=40)	Recreation (n=36)	Environmental (n=27)	Educators (n=10)
Preference for green/ natural appearance	4.36 (.72)	4.27 (.95)	4.11 (.77)	4.31 (.66)	4.36 (.44)	4.40 (.85)
Preference for small, greened-up clearings[†]	3.44 a (.59)	3.26 (.92)	3.70 b (.78)	3.37 c (.80)	2.80 a b c (.64)	3.40 (.61)
Preference for partial retention	2.83 (.97)	.69 (.72)	3.36 a (1.22)	2.91 (.94)	2.26 a (.59)	2.78 (.54)
Preference for large or recent clearings[†]	1.85 a (.91)	1.95 e (1.03)	3.06 a b c d e (1.13)	1.74 b (.79)	1.41 c (.35)	1.53 d (.30)

Note: Means sharing the same letter are significantly different at $p \leq 0.05$.

* Mean preferences, on a 5-point scale with 5 = highest preference.

[†] Dunnet's C post hoc test run.

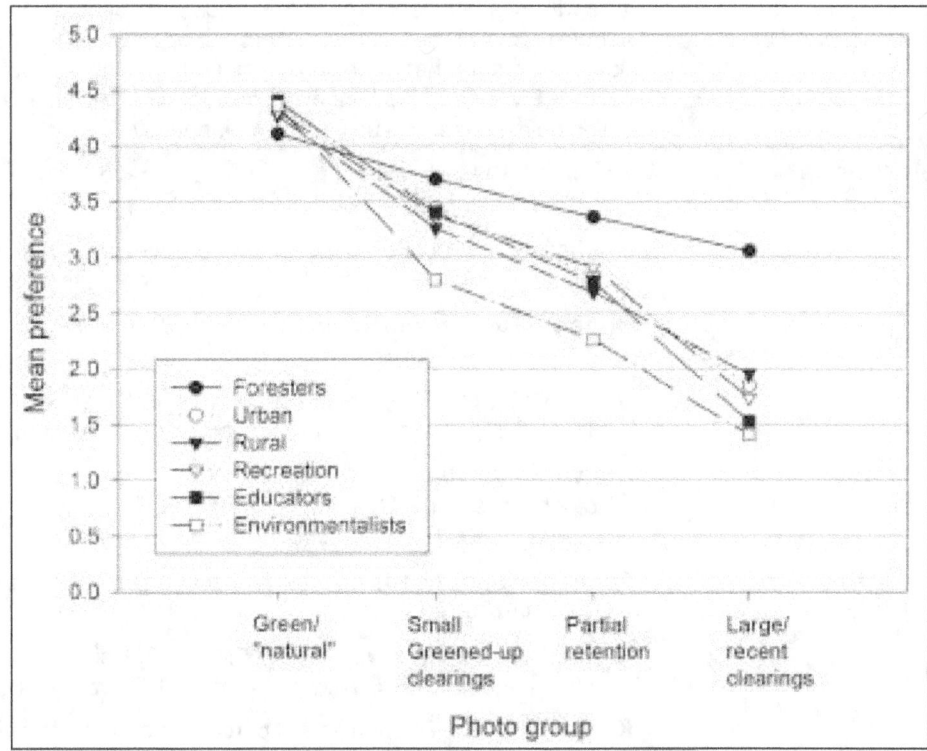

Figure 7-2—Preference for scene type, by population group.

Future Analyses

Subsequent analysis of the Blue Ridge survey data will explore the following:

- Stated rationale behind the preference ratings.
- Knowledge and attitudes toward various aspects of forest management.
- Effect of knowledge and attitudes on preference.
- Correlation of the preference data with biological, economic, and physical data collected by others.

Plans at Blue Ridge

For longitudinal study purposes, we plan to continue collecting photographs of the Blue Ridge site annually. Whereas the initial survey essentially looked at the harvest treatments within a short period, it would be interesting to look at how preferences change over time for each of the individual treatments.

Plans for Copper Ridge

The harvest treatments on the Copper Ridge site will be on sloping terrain, providing opportunities to evaluate visual effects from middle-ground and background distances. This will complement the earlier work of this project on the Blue Ridge site on Capitol Forest where photographs of foreground scenes were collected for treatments on relatively flat terrain.

Selected groups of people will be asked to rate the attractiveness of photographs of alternative timber harvest patterns along with photos of general forest scenes and to explain their reasons for such ratings, including specific elements within the photos and any symbolic meanings associated with the elements.

The initial photos for the Copper Ridge site were taken prior to harvest in spring 2002. This will provide a baseline set of images to be used as control photographs in subsequent surveys as well as the background upon which various treatments will be superimposed. Photographs will be superimposed by using computer manipulation software such as Photoshop. Additional photographs will be taken annually for about 5 years, at which point images will be collected biannually.

References

Bacon, W. 1995. Creating an attractive landscape through viewshed management. Journal of Forestry. 93(2): 26-28.

Bradley, G.A. 1996. Forest aesthetics: harvest practices in visually sensitive areas. Olympia, WA: Washington Forest Protection Association. 21 p.

British Columbia Ministry of Forests. 1981. Forest landscape handbook. Victoria, BC. 100 p.

British Columbia Ministry of Forests. 1994. A first look at visually effective green-up on British Columbia: a public perception study. Victoria, BC. 54 p.

Brown, T.; Daniel, T. 1984. Modeling forest scenic beauty: concepts and applications to ponderosa pine. Res. Pap. RM-RP-256. Fort Collins, CO: U.S. Department of Agriculture, Forest Service, Rocky Mountain Forest and Range Experiment Station. 35 p.

Forestry Authority. 1994. Forest landscape design—guidelines. Wrecclesham, Farnham, Surry, UK: Research Division.

Green, S.B.; Slakind, N.J.; Akey, T.M. 1997. Using SPSS for Windows: analyzing and understanding data. Englewood Cliffs, NJ: Prentice Hall. 494 p.

Kaplan, R. 1985. The analysis of perceptions via preference: a strategy for studying how the environment is experienced. Landscape Planning. 12: 161-176.

Kaplan, R.; Kaplan, S. 1989. The experience of nature: a psychological perspective. New York, NY: Cambridge University Press. 340 p.

Kaplan, R.; Kaplan, S.; Brown, T.J. 1989. Environmental preference: a comparison of four domains of predictors. Environment and Behavior. 21: 509-530.

Lucas, W.R. 1991. The design of forest landscapes. New York: British Forestry Commission, Oxford University Press. 374 p.

Northeast Regional Agricultural Engineering Service. 1993. A guide to logging aesthetics: practical tips for loggers, foresters and landowners. 28 p.

Ribe, R.G. 1989. The aesthetics of forestry: What has empirical reference research taught us? Environmental Management. 13(1): 55-74.

Shelby, B.; Thompson, J.; Brunson, M.; Johnson, R. 2003. Changes in scenic quality after harvest: a decade of ratings for six silviculture treatments. Journal of Forestry. 101(2): 30-35.

SPSS, Inc. 1999. SPSS Base 10.0 applications guide. Chicago, IL: SPSS, Inc. 426 p.

Ulrich, R.S. 1986. Responses to vegetation and landscaping. Landscapes and Urban Planning. 13: 29-44.

U.S. Department of Agriculture, Forest Service. 1974. National Forest landscape management. In: The visual management system. Agric. Handb. 462. Washington, DC. 47 p. Vol. 2.

U.S. Department of Agriculture, Forest Service. 1980. National forest landscape management. In: Timber. Agric. Handb. 559. Washington, DC. 223 p. Vol. 2, Chapter 5.

Zube, H.H.; Pitt, D.G.; Anderson, T.W. 1975. Perception and prediction of scenic resource values of the Northeast. In: Zube, E.H.; Brush, R.O.; Fabos, J.G., eds. Landscape assessment: values, perceptions and resources. Stroudsburg, PA: Dowden, Hutchinson, and Ross: 151-167.

Chapter 8: Economic Analysis

Kevin Zobrist, Michelle Ludwig, and Bruce R. Lippke

In order to compare economic returns for each treatment over time, it is necessary to project treated stands with a growth model. For this study, the stand management cooperative (SMC) variant of ORGANON, an individual tree growth model developed by Oregon State University (Hann et al. 1997), was used to project tree growth and simulate silvicultural treatments. The SMC variant performs best for areas like Blue Ridge that are dominated by Douglas-fir (*Pseudotsuga menziesii* (Mirb.) Franco) and western hemlock (*Tsuga heterophylla* (Raf.) Sarg.).

Growth and Harvest Projections

Running the ORGANON simulations required several assumptions about the continued management scheme for each regime, such as the rotation length and the type and timing of intermediate operations. A 60-year rotation length was used for the clearcut, two-age, and control regimes, and it represents the liquidation period for the patch cut and group selection regimes. The thinning regime represents an extended rotation option. The assumed rotation lengths are not necessarily economically optimal. Rather they are meant to provide consistent comparisons between the treatments. Other rotations may be more appropriate depending on site characteristics, species composition, and specific landowner objectives. The timing and intensity of commercial thinning harvests were guided by relative density goals (Curtis 1982) such that commercial thinning was done when relative density reached 60.

For the clearcut regime projections, a postharvest regeneration tree list was created that consisted of 436 Douglas-fir per acre (approximately a 10-ft by 10-ft spacing) and 10 western redcedar per acre. This regeneration list was based on a nearby stand that was representative of typical Washington Department of Natural Resources (DNR) clearcut regeneration and management. The regeneration list was projected in ORGANON for 60 years to final harvest, with a precommercial thin to 250 trees per acre simulated at age 15 and commercial thins simulated at ages 30 and 45.

The two-age regime is similar to the clearcut treatment, except that approximately 15 trees per acre are left in the residual stand. The residual stand was projected by using a tree list from the posttreatment inventory. Regeneration was simulated by adding an understory at age 15 consisting of 420 Douglas-fir and 16 western redcedar per acre.

To account for reduced growth of the new stand caused by the residual overstory, diameters in the understory tree list were reduced by 40 percent, and the heights were reduced by 30 percent compared to the clearcut treatment. A slightly heavier precommercial thin (to 200 trees per acre) was done at age 15, and the reduced vigor of the new stand (because of the residual overstory) supported only one commercial thin at age 30. Final harvest was simulated at age 60, leaving a new set of 15 trees per acre in the residual stand.

For the patch cut regime, 20 percent of the area is clearcut every 15 years in patches of 1.5 to 5 acres with the matrix thinned as needed. Each component (patches and thinned) of the stand was projected separately and then combined for a stand estimate. The thinned areas were projected from a tree list of the inventory after treatment. In year 30 after the patch cut, the 40 percent of the existing stand that still remains receives a commercial thin. With the first cut occurring in year zero, the fifth and final harvest of the existing timber occurs in year 60. However, the first harvest of the subsequent rotation occurs at year 75, and all subsequent rotations are 75 years. Within each patch, management projections are similar to the clearcut regime, with the same regeneration tree list after harvest as for the clearcut, a precommercial thin at age 15, and a commercial thin at ages 30 and 45. Because the patches are larger than 1 acre, tree growth is assumed to be the same as in a clearcut regime (McDonald and Fiddler 1991).

The group selection regime is similar to the patch cut regime in that 20 percent of the area is harvested every 15 years, and the matrix is thinned as needed. Harvested areas are much smaller, though, ranging from a little over an acre down to single tree selection. Each cutting cycle is projected three ways to represent the appropriate proportions of large (greater than 0.75 acre), medium (0.1 to 0.75 acre), and small (less than 0.1 acre) group selections. The large groups were simulated in the same way as the clearcut and patch cut treatments. The medium groups were expected to have reduced growth because of the edge effect of the residual stand. To account for this, the diameters and heights of the regeneration were reduced by 80 percent in the first 10 years and by 20 percent in the next 5 years. Crown ratios also were adjusted, and mortality was increased. A precommercial thinning was simulated at age 15 for the medium groups, but only one commercial thinning at age 45. Only natural regeneration of shade-tolerant species is modeled for the small groups, with no precommercial or commercial thin. As with the patch area, the different areas within the unit (small, medium, and large groups and the thinned matrix) were projected separately for each cutting cycle and then combined to give stand-level estimates.

For the repeated thinning regime, the existing timber was commercially thinned, and the posttreatment stand inventory was projected in ORGANON for 35 years until a clearcut at age 105. Subsequent rotations were simulated in a way similar to that of the clearcut regime, except that the commercial thins were heavier and the final harvest was done at age 90. This is probably near culmination of mean annual increment, although age of culmination of thinned stands is not well defined.

Finally, the continued regime defers harvest 60 years with no treatment. The existing inventory was projected for 60 years and then clearcut. Subsequently, simulations were done on a 60-year clearcut rotation with no intermediate thinning operations.

Economic Analysis

The net present value (NPV) of cashflows over the next 180 years is used to compare the economic performance of the six regimes. The NPV includes all costs and revenues associated with harvesting the existing timber, plus subsequent estimated revenues and costs out to year 180 discounted back to the year of initial entry (1998) by using a real (no inflation) interest rate of 5 percent.

Looking at the NPV of cashflows allows comparisons of treatment regimes in which cash flows occur at different times and over different rotations. The NPV of cashflows reflects the economic performance of both the liquidation strategy for the existing timber and the management of subsequent rotations. A timeframe of 180 years was chosen for several reasons. One reason is that it was convenient to have an ending year that fell at the end of a rotation for three of the treatments (clearcut, two-age, and control). Another reason is that 180 years is long enough such that cashflows and any residual stand values beyond that period are insignificant ($1 in 180 years is worth less than one-fiftieth of a cent today at a 5 percent interest rate). Thus the NPV of cashflows over 180 years approximates the total economic value of the forest as an asset under a given treatment regime.

The NPV calculations are based on the operational costs described by Reutebuch and Johnson in chapter 5. Log values are based on 1998 prices as reported by Arbor-Pacific Forestry Services (1998). This economic analysis considers timber values only, as we have no basis for assigning dollar values to aesthetic, wildlife, or other social and environmental values associated with the treatments.

Net Present Value Results

The NPV for each regime is plotted in figure 8-1. As expected, the clearcut regime has the highest NPV at $20,936 per acre. The currently standing timber is already economically mature such that the opportunity cost of holding the timber longer at a 5-percent interest rate exceeds the economic gains from additional growth. Thus, the clearcut regime maximizes the present value of the currently standing timber by harvesting all of it immediately. The clearcut regime also has the lowest harvesting costs.

The two-age regime has the next highest NPV at $17,786 per acre, which is a 15-percent reduction from the clearcut regime. The present value of the currently standing timber is diminished by retaining 15 trees per acre through the next rotation. Also, the yield from future harvests is reduced because growth is inhibited by this residual overstory. Harvesting costs are more expensive than with the clearcut regime.

The NPV for the group selection regime is $13,790 per acre, which is a 34-percent reduction from the clearcut treatment. It takes 60 years to liquidate all of the existing timber, which reduces its present value. Future yields also are reduced, as growth is slowed by the residual growing stock compared to the open-grown conditions of the clearcut regime. Harvesting costs are the most expensive with this regime.

The patch cut regime is similar to the group selection regime, but with larger harvest areas. These larger openings allow for faster regeneration growth that is less inhibited by the residual growing stock, and they allow for lower operational costs than does the group selection regime. The NPV under the patch cut regime is $14,255 per acre, which is 32 percent less than the clearcut regime and slightly higher than group selection.

The NPV for the continued thinning regime is $11,808 per acre, a 44-percent reduction from the clearcut treatment. The final harvest of the existing timber is postponed for 35 years, reducing its present value. This is partially mitigated by an initial commercial thin. Subsequent rotations are extended to 90 years, reducing their present value as well.

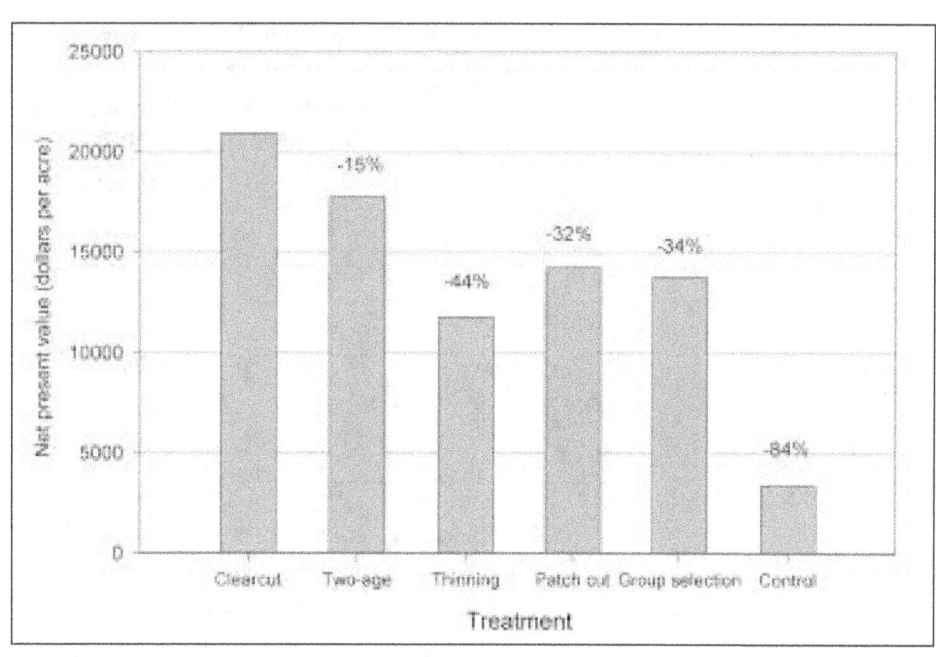

Figure 8-1—Net present value of cashflows for the existing timber and subsequent rotations out to 180 years at a 5-percent discount rate for each treatment regime.

The control regime (extended rotation without thinning) had the lowest NPV at $3,416 per acre, which is an 84-percent reduction compared to the clearcut regime. With the control regime, the existing timber is held for another 60 years after study initiation without intermediate thinnings. This substantially reduces the present value of the currently standing timber. Subsequent rotations are 60 years, similar to those of the clearcut regime, but the subsequent rotations do not contribute much to NPV under this regime because the next rotation does not begin until year 60.

Tradeoff Issues

The visual perception survey described by Bradley et al. (chapter 7) allows for some comparison between the economic performance of each regime and public approval of the resulting aesthetics. These comparisons are somewhat limited for two reasons. The first reason is that there are no data available to assign economic value to a given visual perception rating, so it is not possible to do direct cost-benefit comparisons. The second reason is that the economic figures represent net present values over time, whereas the visual perception survey only measures public approval at a single point in time, which is after the initial treatment. Visual perceptions are likely to change as stands develop.

Despite these limitations, comparisons of economic performance and public approval are still a good illustration of some of the tradeoffs associated with each regime. Table 8-1 lists the NPV and mean visual perception rating for each harvest treatment. This table shows that for most regimes, a marginal improvement in the visual perception rating over another regime comes with a tradeoff of a marginal decrease in the NPV of cashflows. Thus, the control regime, although it has the highest level of public approval, has the lowest NPV. Likewise, the clearcut regime has the highest NPV but the lowest level of public approval. The one exception is the patch cut regime, which is inferior to the two-age regime in NPV but virtually identical in visual perception rating.

Table 8-1—Tradeoffs between public approval and
economic performance of each treatment

Treatment	Mean visual perception rating	Net present value
		Dollars per acre
Clearcut	1.79	20,936
Two-age	2.75	17,786
Patch cut	2.70	14,255
Group selection	2.92	13,790
Thinning	4.04	11,808
Control	4.43	3,416

Table 8-2—Tradeoffs between public approval and economic
performance of each visual characteristic grouping

Visual characteristic	Mean visual perception value	Net present value
		Dollars per acre
Large or recent clearings	2.12	18,006
Partial retention	2.85	17,786
Small, greened-up clearings	3.33	13,284
All green appearance	4.27	8,844

The results of the visual perception survey indicate that respondents did not discriminate between regimes so much as between visual characteristics. With this in mind, it may be more appropriate to compare tradeoffs between these visual characteristics rather than between specific treatment groups. Table 8-2 lists the mean visual perception rating and the mean NPV corresponding to four visual characteristic groupings.

As with the individual regimes, marginal improvements in public approval from one regime to another involve the tradeoff of a decrease in economic performance. It is difficult to directly compare these tradeoffs, as it cannot be assumed that the public perception value scale is linear with the public's willingness to pay for that benefit. However, it is quite evident that the 0.73 improvement in value achieved by partial retention compared to the large clearcut comes at a much smaller cost, $220 per acre, than the next increment of improvement. The improvement provided by small clearings over partial retention, 0.48, comes at an additional cost of $4,502 per acre. The last increment of improvement to an all green appearance compared to the small clearings, 0.94, also comes at a high cost, $4,440 per acre. Ultimately, it is up to policymakers to decide which treatment or group of treatments is most preferable given their respective combinations of benefits and tradeoffs.

References

Arbor-Pacific Forestry Services. 1998. Log lines, log price reporting service. Mt. Vernon, WA. Log Lines. 10(12): 1-8.

Curtis, R.O. 1982. A simple index of stand density for Douglas-fir. Forest Science. 28: 92-94.

Hann, D.W.; Hester, A.S.; Olsen, C.L. 1997. ORGANON users manual: edition 6.0. Corvallis, OR: Department of Forest Resources, Oregon State University. 113 p.

McDonald, P.M.; Fiddler, G.O. 1991. Vegetation in group selection opening: ecology and manipulation. In: Proceedings, 12th annual forest vegetation management conference. Redding, CA: Shasta County Opportunity Center: 97-106.

Chapter 9: Spring Bird Survey and Social Perceptions

Todd M. Wilson, Andrew B. Carey, and Bruce A. Haveri

Introduction

Controversy over timber harvesting practices has increased, and public perception of forest management has become an increasingly important factor in defining and resolving conflicts over land management decisions. In contrast to mixed attitudes toward timber harvesting, most people are favorably disposed toward wildlife and the welfare of wild animals. However, the public often has little knowledge about the relationship between forest structure and wildlife habitat, and how different stages of forest development can influence (both positively and negatively) wildlife habitat. Bird calls and songs have potential in interpretive programs to educate the public through experiential learning about effects of forest practices, and to engage the public in evaluation of forestry practices in collaborative management efforts.

Birds are highly valued by much of the public because they contribute to the aesthetics of a forest experience. Both the number of people and proportion of the population that participate in wildlife watching (feeding, observing, or photographing wildlife) as a recreational activity in the United States have increased dramatically (Aiken 1999). There is substantial public support for migratory songbirds, and they are readily recognizable by their songs as well as by behavior and appearance. Thus, birds may provide an important and effective communication link between forest managers and the public.

In Pacific Northwest forests, birds are usually heard but not seen. Even though some forest birds are very colorful (e.g., some finches and warblers), they are small and often hidden in the canopy or understory and cannot be easily observed. In contrast, people readily cue in to bird songs, even if they cannot identify the species. Both species abundance and species composition may be important in contributing to an aesthetic forest experience. For example, the breeding call of varied thrushes (see table 9-1 for scientific names of bird species) or hermit warblers may be perceived as melodious but the sounds from American crows or Steller's jays as raucous. Thus, silvicultural treatments with high numbers of thrushes or assemblages of warbler species may positively influence public perceptions.

Table 9-1—All bird species found across six treatment units, Blue Ridge study area, from 12 April to 11 June, 1999

Common name	Scientific name
American robin	*Turdus migratorius* (Linnaeus 1766)
Band-tailed pigeon	*Columba fasciata* (Say 1823)
Bewick's wren	*Thryomanes bewickii* (Audubon 1827)
Black-capped chickadee	*Parus atricapillus* (Linnaeus 1766)
Black-headed grosbeak	*Pheucticus melanocephalus* (Swainson 1827)
Black-throated gray warbler	*Dendroica nigrescens* (Townsend 1837)
Blue grouse	*Dendragapus obscurus* (Roman 1823)
Brown creeper	*Certhia americana* (Bonaparte 1838)
Cassin's vireo	*Vireo cassinii* (Xantus de Vesey 1858)
Chestnut-backed chickadee	*Parus rufescens* (Townsend 1837)
Common nighthawk	*Chordeiles minor* (Forster 1771)
Common raven	*Corvus corax* (Linnaeus 1758)
Dark-eyed junco	*Junco hyemalis organus* (Linnaeus 1758)
Downy woodpecker	*Picoides pubescens* (Linnaeus 1766)
Evening grosbeak	*Coccothraustes vespertinus* (Cooper 1825)
Golden-crowned kinglet	*Regulus saltrapa* (Lichtenstein 1823)
Golden-crowned sparrow	*Zonotrichia atricapilla* (Gmelin 1789)
Gray jay	*Perisoreus canadensis* (Linnaeus 1766)
Hairy woodpecker	*Picoides villosus* (Linnaeus 1766)
Hermit thrush	*Catharus guttatus* (Pallas 1811)
Hermit warbler	*Dendroica occidentalis* (Townsend 1837)
Hermit x Townsend's warbler	see hermit or Townsend's warbler
Hutton's vireo	*Vireo huttoni* (Cassin 1851)
MacGillivray's warbler	*Oporornis tolmiei* (Townsend 1837)
Mountain bluebird	*Sialia currucoides* (Bechstein 1798)
Mourning dove	*Zenaida macroura* (Linnaeus 1758)
Northern flicker	*Colaptes auratus* (Linnaeus 1758)
Northern saw-whet owl	*Aegolius acadicus* (Gmelin 1788)
Orange-crowned warbler	*Vermivora celata* (Say 1823)
Pacific-slope flycatcher	*Empidonax difficilis* (Baird 1858)
Pileated woodpecker	*Drycopus pileatus* (Linnaeus 1758)

Table 9-1—All bird species found across six treatment units, Blue Ridge study area, from 12 April to 11 June, 1999 (continued)

Common name	Scientific name
Pine siskin	*Carduelis pinus* (Wilson 1810)
Purple finch	*Carpodacus purpureus* (Gmelin 1789)
Red-breasted nuthatch	*Sitta canadensis* (Linnaeus 1766)
Red-breasted sapsucker	*Sphyrapicus ruber* (Gmelin 1788)
Red-tailed hawk	*Buteo jamaicensis* (Gmelin 1788)
Ruby-crowned kinglet	*Regulus calendula* (Linnaeus 1766)
Rufous hummingbird	*Selasphorus rufus* (Gmelin 1788)
Sharp-shinned hawk	*Accipiter striatus* (Vieillot 1807)
Song sparrow	*Melospiza melodia* (Wilson 1810)
Spotted towhee	*Pipilo maculatus* (Swainson 1827)
Steller's jay	*Cyanocitta stelleri* (Gmelin 1788)
Swainson's thrush	*Catharus ustulatus* (Nuttal 1840)
Townsend's solitaire	*Myadestes townsendi* (Audubon 1838)
Townsend's warbler	*Dendroica townsendi* (Townsend 1837)
Varied thrush	*Ixoreus naevius* (Gmelin 1789)
Western tanager	*Piranga ludoviciana* (Wilson 1811)
White-crowned sparrow	*Zonotrichia leucophrys* (Forster 1772)
Willow flycatcher	*Empidonax traillii* (Audubon 1828)
Wilson's warbler	*Wilsonia pusilla* (Wilson 1811)
Winter wren	*Troglodytes troglodytes* (Linnaeus 1758)

Source of scientific names: American Ornithologists' Union 1998.

The silvicultural options for young-growth Douglas-fir forests study was designed to evaluate alternative operational-scale regeneration harvests in second-growth Douglas-fir (*Pseudotsuga menziesii* (Mirb.) Franco) forests for economic and biological consequences, and for acceptability to the public (Curtis et al. 1997). The study site is near both urban and rural communities and thus provides a cost-effective opportunity to evaluate public response to alternative harvests from a wide range of user groups.

An objective of the study was to evaluate silvicultural regimes that could be used to reduce negative visual impressions (and thus negative public perceptions) of timber management operations while maintaining a high level of timber production. It was recognized, however, that public perception of forest management includes factors other than visual impressions. Factors such as frequency and variety of bird songs and calls may be important components influencing human experience and perceptions of managed forests.

A long-term objective of the study is to create methods by which the public can interact with and understand modern concepts of management of forest ecosystems. Little empirical data exist on the value of natural cues to aesthetic experience or their use in interpretive programs. Furthermore, few prospective studies of silvicultural options have been conducted in second-growth conifer forests that include measurements of aesthetics.

We initiated the Capitol Forest bird study in 1999 to evaluate the effectiveness of birds as an interpretive tool for land managers evaluating public perception of alternative forest management strategies. The overall objectives of this study are the following:

- Determine how songbird abundance and community structure respond, over time, to six silvicultural treatments.

- Measure the degree to which changes in avian communities are reflected in frequency and variety of calls and songs.

- Measure public response to songbird frequency and variety.

- Measure the public acceptability of six silvicultural treatments 1 to 3 years after harvest.

- Measure the extent to which songbird abundance and other effects of the silvicultural treatments modify public acceptability of the treatments.

Thus, the study consists of two broad components: (1) a biotic component that evaluates the response of songbird communities (structure and abundance) to six treatments and (2) a social component that measures the public response to treatments.

In this report, we present the results from our first year of evaluating the biotic component (e.g., birds) and begin to evaluate three hypotheses:

1. Treatments will increase landscape-level and stand-level songbird diversity and abundance.

2. Treatments will increase within-stand songbird species richness and abundance.

3. Increased avian abundance and diversity will be apparent to the public through increased frequency and variety of bird calls and songs.

Avian response to silvicultural treatments of managed forests in the Pacific Northwest has been well documented. Studies of breeding and wintering birds in southeast Alaska (DellaSalla et al. 1996), the Coast Ranges of Oregon (Chambers and McComb 1997, Chambers et al. 1999, Hagar et al. 1996) and the Puget Trough of Washington (Haveri and Carey 2000) suggest greater overall abundance and species richness in thinned stands than in clearcuts or closed-canopy even-aged stands.

Our objectives for the initial biotic evaluation were to collect, analyze, and summarize early posttreatment bird community data to determine if songs and calls differed significantly between treatments. If songs and calls are of sufficient frequency and variety in at least some treatments, they may be useful in (1) interpretive programs on forest management to educate the public, (2) public evaluation of forest management alternatives, and (3) assessment of the relative ecological value of forest management alternatives.

Study Area and Methods

The study was initiated in 1997 with the selection of the first block of regimes, the Blue Ridge study site, located in Capitol State Forest approximately 15 miles southwest of Olympia, Washington, in the southern Puget Trough Physiographic Province (Franklin and Dyrness 1973). The forest is managed by the Black Hills District of the Washington Department of Natural Resources. The study area encompasses approximately 300 acres and includes six treatment units ranging from 30 to 80 acres. Regimes (silvicultural options) include extended rotation without thinning (control), extended rotation with repeated thinning, group selection, patch cut, two-age, and clearcut. Residual portions (i.e., areas outside the patches and groups) in the group selection and patch cut also were thinned. Treatment units were harvested in spring and summer 1998. Study area and harvest treatments are fully described by Curtis, DeBell, and DeBell (chapter 2) and Curtis et al. (chapter 3).

Bird Sampling

We used a 131.2-ft (40-m) fixed-radius point count method (Hutto et al. 1986, Manuwal and Carey 1991) to estimate abundance and diversity of birds from April to June 1999. We chose this method for several reasons: (1) we planned to compare abundances among very different habitat types (from clearcuts to closed-canopy second-growth forests); (2) individual treatment units were small relative to bird movements, and we wanted to reduce influence from outside the treatments as much as possible; and (3) most common species west of the Cascade Range have an effective detection distance of 164 ft (50 m) or less (Carey et al. 1991). Thirty-four point count stations were systematically located about 295 ft (90 m) apart at existing permanent plot markers. Stations were at least 328 ft (100 m) from treatment boundaries or untreated riparian reserves. Thus four to nine stations were systematically distributed in each of the six treatments (fig. 9-1). Surveys began within 20 minutes of sunrise and concluded by 10:00 a.m. daily. All 34 stations were surveyed each morning. Each station was visited 15 times (5 visits each by 3 observers), once each day for 5 days each during April, May, and June 1999. We did not survey during periods of moderate to heavy rain, in foggy conditions, or when winds exceeded 15 mph (25 kph).

At each count station the station number and time were recorded (fig. 9-2). Observers began counts immediately upon reaching the station center, and continued for 8 minutes. We recorded bird data in five basic categories: species and number of individuals <66 ft (20 m) from the station, 66 to 131 ft (20 to 40 m) from the station, more than 131 ft (40 m) from the station, flyovers that did not land within 131 ft (40 m) of the station, and

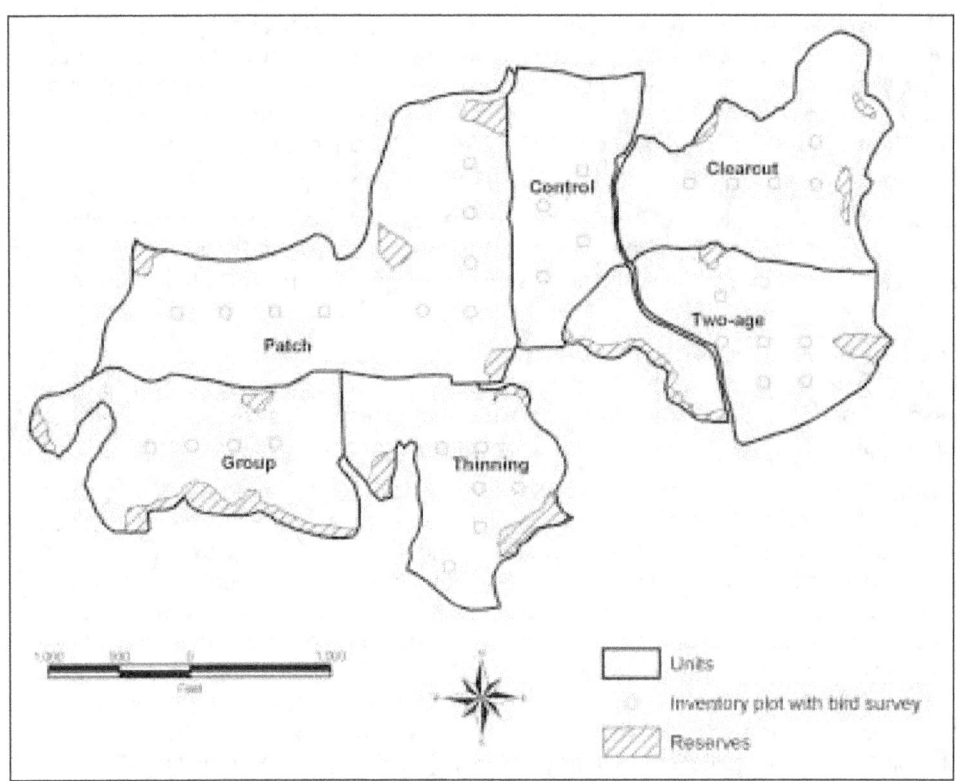

Figure 9-1—Locations of bird count stations.

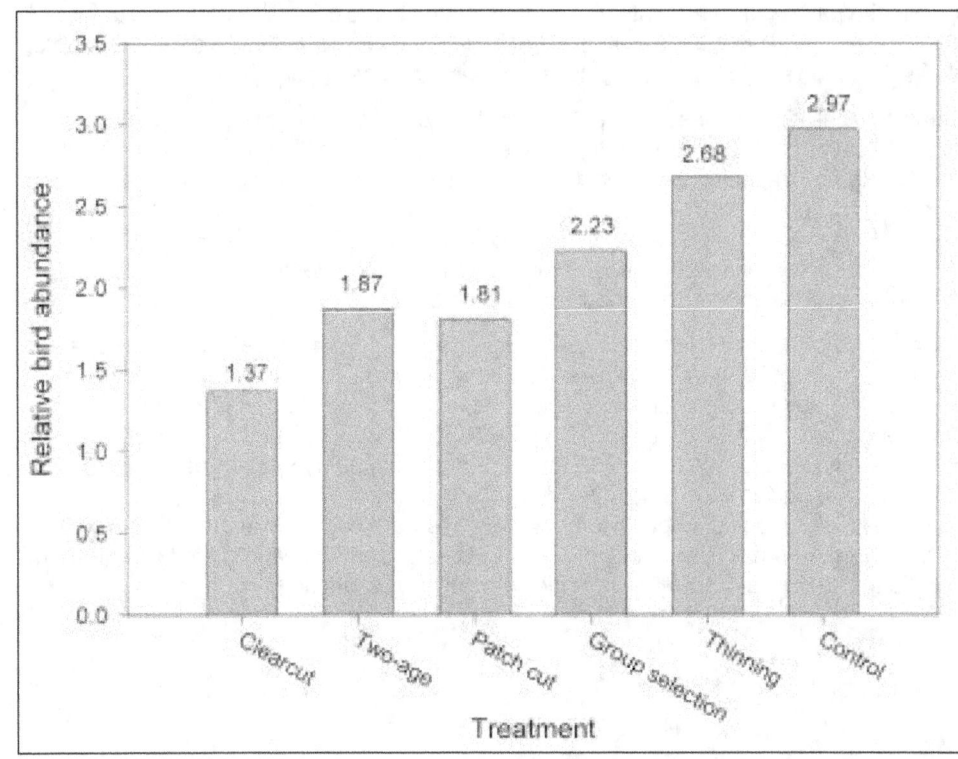

Figure 9-2—Bird abundance (mean number of birds detected per point per day), by treatment regime.

detection cue (visual, song, call, or flush) for each species. Additionally, we recorded birds that flushed between stations if they were not detected from a station. Flushed birds, flyovers, and birds detected beyond the 131-ft (40 m) radius were recorded to develop a species list, but were not used to compare treatments. Birds detected outside the 131-ft radius boundary that moved to within 131 ft of the observer during the count period were recorded as occurring within the fixed-radius circle.

Observers noted locations of flushing birds while approaching the station, then determined the distance to flush point after reaching the station center. Birds that flushed from within the fixed-radius circle while the observer was approaching the station were included in the data.

Flocks or individual birds detected within the circle but unidentified before the end of the 8-minute count period were pursued (if still visible or audible) for up to 10 minutes after the count period for identification. New birds detected during this time were treated as birds flushed between stations and recorded as present only.

Data Analysis

The guidelines of Hutto et al. (1986) were generally followed to develop indices of abundance from fixed-radius count data. Owing to (1) differences in the number of count stations per treatment (and thus time spent listening for birds), (2) the proximity of count stations within treatment units, and (3) the high mobility of birds, count stations were not considered independent samples. Therefore, detections (both bird counts and species counts) were averaged across stations to derive a daily detection rate (mean number of detections per point per day) for each treatment. We calculated treatment means and standard errors for each species and for overall abundance (species combined). Means generated in this fashion account for variances in detection (primarily songs) owing to breeding phenology (different species establishing territories at different times throughout the spring), and begin to address differences in sampling effort (for example, nine stations in the patch-cut treatment versus four stations in the control treatment). All analysis was performed with SPSS version 10.0 software (Norusis 1999). Except where noted, all results reported are from 131-ft (40-m) fixed-radius point count data.

Results

Between April 12 and June 11, 1999, we made 510 visits to 34 stations in the 6 treatment units. We counted 1,070 birds representing 42 species (31 year-round resident and 11 migratory species including 1 hybrid) within 131 ft (40 m) of station centers, while recording a total of 2,169 birds of 51 species (38 resident and 13 migratory species including 1 hybrid) during unlimited distance point counts (table 9-1). Twenty-one species (15 resident and 6 migratory species) with more than five detections each made up 96 percent of all birds counted in fixed-radius treatments.

Relative Abundance

Overall bird abundance (mean number of birds detected per point per day) differed among treatment units and generally followed degree of disturbance caused by timber harvest activities. Relative abundance was highest in the control unit (2.97±0.29) and lowest in the clearcut unit (1.37±0.17; table 9-2; fig. 9-2). The control unit had the highest percentage of relative abundance (table 9-3) for the 10 most abundant species combined. Four of the top ten species were most often found in the control (brown creeper, golden-crowned kinglet, Pacific-slope flycatcher, Wilson's warbler), three in the commercial thin (winter wren, American robin, and evening grosbeak), and one each in the two-age (dark-eyed junco) and clearcut (white-crowned sparrow) treatment unit.

Table 9-2—Relative abundance (RA)[a] ± 1 standard error for all bird species detected within 131 ft (40 m) of point stations in 6 treatments, Blue Ridge study area from 12 April to 11 June, 1999

Species	Clearcut	Two-age	Patch cut	Group selection	Thinning	Control
American robin	0.05±0.02	0.16±0.10	0.18±0.04	0.10±0.05	0.24±0.06	0.18±0.08
Band-tailed pigeon	—	—	.01±.01	—	—	—
Black-capped chickadee	—	—	.01±.01	.10±.06	.13±.07	.13±.06
Black-headed grosbeak	.01±.01	—	—	—	.01±.01	—
Black-throated gray warbler	—	—	—	—	.01±.01	.02±.02
Blue grouse	—	—	—	—	—	.03±.02
Brown creeper	—	.06±.05	.08±.02	.15±.06	.08±.03	.20±.06
Chestnut-backed chickadee	—	.02±.02	.04±.04	—	.11±.05	—
Common raven	—	—	—	—	.01±.01	—
Dark-eyed junco	.40±.12	.70±.14	.16±.04	.17±.07	.10±.05	—
Downy woodpecker	—	.03±.02	.01±.01	.10±.06	.08±.04	—
Evening grosbeak	—	—	.03±.02	.08±.08	.18±.08	—
Golden-crowned kinglet	—	—	.09±.07	.12±.07	.02±.02	.30±.20
Golden-crowned sparrow	—	.04±.03	—	—	—	—
Gray jay	—	—	.04±.02	.02±.02	.02±.02	.03±.03
Hairy woodpecker	—	.04±.02	.03±.01	.02±.02	.04±.02	.02±.02
Hermit thrush	—	—	—	—	.01±.01	—
Hermit warbler	—	—	—	.05±.03	—	—
Hermit x Townsend's warbler	—	—	.04±.03	—	—	—
Hutton's vireo	—	—	—	—	.02±.02	.02±.02
MacGillivary's warbler	—	.02±.02	—	—	—	—
Mountain bluebird	.01±.01	—	—	—	—	—

Table 9-2—Relative abundance (RA)[a] ± 1 standard error for all bird species detected within 131 ft (40 m) of point stations in 6 treatments, Blue Ridge study area from 12 April to 11 June, 1999 (continued)

Species	Clearcut	Two-age	Patch cut	Group selection	Thinning	Control
Northern flicker	.01±.01	.01±.01	—	—	—	—
Orange-crowned warbler	—	—	—	.02±.02	.01±.01	.03±.02
Pacific-slope flycatcher	—	—	.04±.02	.07±.03	.08±.03	.33±.08
Red-breasted nuthatch	—	—	.01±.01	—	—	—
Red-breasted sapsucker	—	.01±.02	.02±.02	—	—	—
Ruby-crowned kinglet	—	—	—	—	.01±.01	—
Rufous hummingbird	.04±.02	.03±.02	.02±.01	.02±.02	.04±.03	.02±.02
Sharp-shinned hawk	—	—	—	—	.01±.01	—
Song sparrow	.01±.01	—	—	—	—	—
Spotted towhee	.13±.04	.03±.02	—	—	.01±.01	.02±.02
Steller's jay	—	—	.01±.01	.03±.03	.02±.02	—
Swainson's thrush	—	—	.01±.01	—	—	.02±.02
Townsend's solitaire	.04±.04	—	—	—	—	—
Townsend's warbler	—	—	.01±.01	—	.07±.06	—
Varied thrush	—	—	.01±.01	.02±.02	—	.23±.10
Western tanager	—	—	—	.02±.02	.08±.03	—
White-crowned sparrow	.35±.1	.11±.04	—	—	—	—
Willow flycatcher	.01±.01	—	—	—	—	—
Wilson's warbler	—	.07±.05	.04±.02	.08±.07	.04±.03	.23±.08
Winter wren	.27±.04	.52±.06	.88±.06	1.08±.10	1.22±.11	1.15±.13

[a] Mean number of birds detected per point per day for each treatment.

Table 9-3—Percentage of relative abundance (PRA)[a] of the 10 most common species (25 or more detections each) across the 6 treatments, Blue Ridge study area, from 12 April to 11 June, 1999, ordered by average relative abundance (ARA)[b]

Species	Average relative abundance	Percentage of relative abundance					
		Clearcut	Two-age	Patch cut	Group selection	Thinning	Control
Winter wren	0.85	5	10	17	21	24	22
Dark-eyed junco	.26	26	46	10	11	7	0
American robin	.15	5	18	20	11	26	20
Brown creeper	.10	0	11	14	26	14	35
Golden-crowned kinglet	.09	0	0	17	23	4	57
Pacific slope flycatcher	.09	0	0	8	13	15	63
White-crowned sparrow	.08	76	24	0	0	0	0
Wilson's warbler	.08	0	15	9	17	9	50
Black-capped chickadee	.06	0	0	3	27	35	35
Evening grosbeak	.05	0	0	10	28	62	0

[a] PRA = 100 $(RA_i / \Sigma (RA_i))$ where RA_i = relative abundance (mean number of birds detected per point per day).

[b] ARA = $\Sigma (RA_i) / 6$, where RA_i = relative abundance (mean number of birds detected per point per day).

Species Richness

Species richness differed among treatments but was, in part, confounded by treatment unit size and number of sampling points (e.g., the more points sampled and area covered, the more likelihood of encountering additional species; figs. 9-1 and 9-2). The highest number of species was found in the commercial thin treatment (n = 26), followed by the patch cut (n = 22), group selection (n = 18), control (n = 17), two-age (n = 15), and clear-cut treatment units (n = 12). However, on a per sampling point basis, the group selection treatment had the highest average (five species per point), followed by commercial thin (four species per point), control (four species per point), two-age (three species per point), patch cut (two species per point), and clearcut (one species per point). Thirteen species were unique to a single treatment—all were rare. The clearcut treatment had the most unique species—four.

Seven species each accounted for >5 percent of the population (by total count) in the control treatment, whereas only three to four species each accounted for >5 percent in the other five treatments (table 9-4). Additionally, the rank order of relative abundance differed among treatments. The winter wren, ranked highest overall among the treatments, dropped off in importance in the two-age and clearcut treatments (tables 9-3 and 9-4). The dark-eyed junco, ranked highest in the two-age and clearcut treatments, was not observed in the control and accounted for <5 percent of the detections in the commercial thin treatment. Thus, bird community composition differed among the six treatments.

Table 9-4—Most common birds[a] at Blue Ridge Study area, April 12 to June 11, 1999, by treatment

Rank[b]	Clearcut	Two-age	Patch cut	Group selection	Thinning	Control
1	Dark-eyed junco	Dark-eyed junco	Winter wren	Winter wren	Winter wren	Winter wren
2	White-crowned sparrow	Winter wren	American robin	Dark-eyed junco	American robin	Pacific-slope flycatcher
3	Winter wren	American robin	Dark-eyed junco	Brown creeper	Evening grosbeak	Golden-crowned kinglet
4	Spotted towhee	White-crowned sparrow		Golden-crowned kinglet		Wilson's warbler
5						Varied thrush
6						Brown creeper
7						American robin

[a] Species that account for more than 5 percent of the individual birds counted per treatment within 40 meters of point stations.
[b] Rank is based on relative abundance: mean number of birds detected per day for each treatment.

Ten common (>25 total detections each) species made up 82.8 percent of all detections. Six of these species—winter wrens, dark-eyed juncos, brown creepers, Pacific-slope flycatchers, white-crowned sparrows, and Wilson's warblers—differed in abundance among treatments (table 9-2). American robins did not differ among treatments, and golden-crowned kinglets, black-capped chickadees, and evening grosbeaks were not found in either the clearcut treatment or the two-age treatment and had few detections in other treatments. Only three species were detected within fixed-radius boundaries across all treatments: winter wrens, American robins, and rufous hummingbirds.

Winter wrens were the most frequently encountered species and accounted for more than 40 percent of all birds counted. Abundance of winter wrens differed among treatments with four or more times as many wrens detected in control, commercial thin, and group selection units than in the clearcut. Brown creepers were most often detected in the control unit and were not detected in the clearcut unit. Pacific-slope flycatchers were far more abundant in the control treatment than any other treatment and were not detected in the clearcut or two-age treatments. Wilson's warblers were most abundant in the control treatment and absent in the clearcut treatment. Dark-eyed juncos were the most abundant species in both the clearcut treatment and the two-age treatment, whereas no juncos were detected in the control treatment. White-crowned sparrows were found only in the clearcut and two-age treatments. They were the second most abundant species in the clearcut treatment, after dark-eyed juncos.

Bird Patterns and Public Perceptions

Data presented here are observational and limited to a single season and one small geographic area and forest type. Point count census methods are constrained in that only birds that make noise or show themselves are counted. Nevertheless, point counts have been demonstrated to provide accurate representation of passerine birds in forest communities, and these birds would be the ones most apparent to the public. Fixed-radius methods may reduce instances of counting the same bird repeatedly, and thus provide more accurate data than unlimited-distance counts, but may underrepresent rare, cryptic, or shy species. However, we feel these methods sufficiently sampled the variety of habitats in the study area to compare treatments.

Community Patterns

Bird species differ in their habitat requirements, and requirements change seasonally for many species. We therefore expected composition of bird communities to differ among harvest treatments. Although we did not measure specific habitat variables, both abundance and species richness appeared to decline initially relative to the control treatment, in treatments with greater disturbance from timber harvest activities (i.e., clearcut and two-age treatments). This short-term response to habitat disruption likely will reverse as plant communities respond to changes to the ecosystem brought on by the disturbance. Chambers et al. (1999), in a study comparing the effects of three levels of disturbance intensity (small patch cuts, overstory retention, and modified clearcuts), found that bird abundance declined 1 year posttreatment, and then increased during the second and third years following treatment. Haveri and Carey (2000) reported increased species richness and greater use of thinned stands over unthinned stands by resident birds 3 to 6 years after thinning in 60- to 70-year-old Douglas-fir forests in the Puget Trough of Washington. Similarly, Hagar et al. (1996) found bird abundance to be greater in commercially thinned than in unthinned stands 5 to 15 years after thinning in 40- to 55-year-old Douglas-fir forests in the Oregon Coast Range.

Species Patterns

The most abundant species in the least disturbed treatments (control and commercial thin) were all less abundant in the more heavily harvested treatments. Two species displayed the opposite trend: dark-eyed juncos and white-crowned sparrows were both much more prevalent in the clearcut and two-age treatments than in other treatments. Dark-eyed juncos are forest habitat generalists (Ehrlich et al. 1988) and have been found to be more abundant in recently thinned than in unthinned second-growth Douglas-fir forests in the Pacific Northwest (Chambers et al. 1999, Hagar et al. 1996). Chambers et al. (1999) also found white-crowned sparrows to be more abundant in modified clearcuts and two-story stands than in patch cut or control stands in Oregon, suggesting this species prefers more open habitats.

Winter wrens are cavity-nesting ground foragers and are strongly associated with heavy understory cover (Ehrlich et al. 1988). Their reduced presence in clearcut and two-age treatments likely is due to reduction of low cover and suitable cavities. Density of low shrub cover probably will increase dramatically in all but the control treatment over the next couple of years as a result of thinning, and populations of winter wrens should increase over time. The remaining species for which we had sufficient detections (brown creepers, Pacific-slope flycatchers, Wilson's warblers) were all at their greatest abundance in the control treatment and absent from the clearcut treatment.

Variation in bird community composition between the control treatment and other treatments suggests that, for some species, there is varying resiliency to the management activity that occurred on these sites. Overall, in the short term, there appeared to be a tradeoff owing to the disturbance effects of timber harvest activities; the addition of more open habitat through the removal or partial removal of the canopy immediately benefited some species like the white-crowned sparrow, but the reduction of understory owing to disturbance of the forest floor by heavy equipment reduced habitat for ground-dwelling birds like winter wrens. We would expect bird species richness to increase over the next several years in all of the treatments as both the understory and overstory respond to these treatments (increasing plant species richness resulting in a diversity of food sources, increasing density of understory that will provide hiding cover and nest sites, continued progression of decadence in the overstory trees that will provide cavities, etc.). We predict this increase in species richness would be greatest in the patch cut and group selection where the mosaic of forest and small clearings could create a heterogeneous landscape of a scale appropriate to create a variety of habitat niches for different bird species. It is clear that, for the species and area studied, a greater landscape diversity can result from a greater array of stand conditions.

Public Perceptions

Developing an interpretive program around bird songs and measuring the public's response to harvest treatments requires that the public be able to perceive differences in bird cues among treatments. There were clearly empirical differences in both bird abundance and species richness among some treatments. The question is whether these differences are meaningful to the public.

Auditory cues accounted for most observations during the study period, as is typical for most bird surveys in Pacific Northwest forests during the breeding season. Therefore, a focus on auditory cues in building an interpretive program appears more promising than a focus on visual cues alone. On field trips to forested study sites in the Pacific Northwest, participants from a wide range of academic, professional, and technical backgrounds have repeatedly been very attracted to (or distracted by) aural cues emitted by birds, even though these birds are seldom visible (personal observations).

Just as important as differences in species richness, abundance, or composition are in developing an interpretive program, is the ability of the public to perceive these differences while walking through the treatments. Beta-level diversity, diversity between any two treatments, defines the relative differences between treatments and is the basis for forming opinions about the acceptability of treatments. Our data suggest that detection of differences between two treatments is possible, particularly between extreme harvest intensities (clearcut and control) but also likely, for example, between the patch cut and two-age treatments. The order of treatments visited, however, may influence decisions (e.g., extreme differences between adjacent stands may affect opinions more strongly); thus beta-level differences in quantity of bird cues will need to be addressed in the design of the interpretive program. Additionally, because treatment units differ in size, perceived differences in species richness could occur depending on observer route and time spent in each treatment. To compensate for this, interpretive trails of similar lengths could be built in each treatment.

Future Direction

The empirical data to date show that there are differences in both bird abundance and richness among stands 1 year after harvest. We hypothesize that these differences can be perceived in the field by the public and can be used in an interpretive program on timber harvest practices in the Pacific Northwest. We hope to test these hypotheses in the next few years, when even more dramatic differences in bird community structure among treatments are expected and when additional replicates become available. We also hope to study the reaction of both birds and people as conditions change. In fact, people's acceptance of harvesting may well depend on their understanding of the trajectory of conditions created by various harvest methods. The avian and social components of the Capitol Forest bird study will provide direct feedback to scientists and managers concerning how the public perceives management options—not only how songbird populations can be affected by management, but also how an informed public will respond to these effects.

References

Aiken, R. 1999. 1980-1995 participation in fishing, hunting, and wildlife watching: national and regional demographic trends. Report 96-5. Washington, DC: U.S. Fish and Wildlife Service. 84 p.

American Ornithologists' Union. 1998. Check-list of North American birds. 7th ed. Washington, DC: Committee on Classification and Nomenclature. 829 p.

Carey, A.B.; Hardt, M.M.; Horton, S.P.; Biswell, B.L. 1991. Spring bird communities in the Oregon Coast Range. In: Ruggiero, L.F.; Aubry, K.B.; Carey, A.B.; Huff, M.H., tech. coords. Wildlife and vegetation of unmanaged Douglas-fir forests. Gen. Tech. Rep. PNW-GTR-285. Portland, OR: U.S. Department of Agriculture, Forest Service, Pacific Northwest Research Station: 122-142.

Chambers, C.L.; McComb, W.C. 1997. Effects of silvicultural treatments on wintering bird communities in the Oregon Coast Range. Northwest Science. 71: 298-304.

Chambers, C.L.; McComb, W.C.; Tappeiner, J.C., II. 1999. Breeding bird responses to three silvicultural treatments in the Oregon Coast Range. Ecological Applications. 9: 171-185.

Curtis, R.O.; DeBell, D.S.; DeBell, J.D. [et al.]. 1997. Silvicultural options for harvesting young-growth production forests. Study plan on file with: Forestry Sciences Laboratory, 3625 93rd Avenue SW, Olympia, WA 98512-9193.

DellaSala, D.A.; Hagar, J.C.; Engel, K.A. [et al.]. 1996. Effects of silvicultural modifications of temperate rainforest on breeding and wintering bird communities, Prince of Wales Island, southeast Alaska. Condor. 98: 706-721.

Ehrlich, P.R.; Dobkin, D.S.; Wheye, D. 1988. Birder's handbook: a field guide to the natural history of North American birds. New York, NY: Simon and Schuster, Inc. 785 p.

Franklin, J.F.; Dyrness, C.T. 1973. Natural vegetation of Oregon and Washington. Gen. Tech. Rep. PNW-GTR-8. Portland, OR: U.S. Department of Agriculture, Forest Service, Pacific Northwest Forest and Range Experiment Station. 417 p.

Hagar, J.C.; McComb, W.C.; Emmingham, W.H. 1996. Bird communities in commercially thinned and unthinned Douglas-fir stands of western Oregon. Wildlife Society Bulletin. 24: 353-366.

Haveri, B.A.; Carey, A.B. 2000. Forest management strategy, spatial heterogeneity, and winter birds in Washington. Wildlife Society Bulletin. 28: 643-652.

Hutto, R.L.; Pletschet, S.; Hendricks, M.P. 1986. A fixed-radius point count method for nonbreeding and breeding season use. Auk. 103: 593-602.

Manuwal, D.A.; Carey, A.B. 1991. Methods for measuring populations of small, diurnal forest birds. Gen. Tech. Rep. PNW-GTR-278. Portland, OR: U.S. Department of Agriculture, Forest Service, Pacific Northwest Research Station. 23 p.

Norusis, M.J. 1999. SPSS for Windows, Release 10.0. Chicago, IL: SPSS Inc. 535 p.

Chapter 10: Evaluation of Laser Light Detection and Ranging Measurements in a Forested Area[1]

Stephen E. Reutebuch, Hans-Erik Andersen, Kamal Ahmed, and Terry A. Curtis

Introduction

Airborne laser scanning technology is a remote sensing technology that is increasingly being used to map terrain surfaces. This measurement technology uses a laser light detection and ranging (LIDAR) system to compute distances from the airborne sensor to surfaces below the aircraft. As the aircraft flies over an area, the LIDAR system emits laser pulses that are reflected by vegetation, buildings, or the ground surface. A detector in the LIDAR sensor records the time it takes for each laser pulse to travel from the sensor to the ground and back to the sensor. This time is then used to compute the distance from the sensor to the reflecting surface. In open areas with hard surfaces, LIDAR systems often achieve vertical accuracies of 6 inches or better. However, in forested environments covered with dense canopy, the accuracy of LIDAR measurements has not been thoroughly examined.

A LIDAR system was used to scan the surface of the 2 square miles that encompass the Blue Ridge study site (fig.10-1). The forest canopy within the study area is primarily coniferous and highly variable. It included recent clearcuts and forest plantations ranging from recently planted to 70-year-old mature forests. In addition, 108 fixed-radius plots (1/5 acre) were located throughout the study site (fig. 3-1 in chapter 3). The location of each plot was established with either global positioning system (GPS) receivers or ground survey methods (Reutebuch et al. 2000). On each plot all trees were measured, and a subsample of groundcover vegetation was collected both prior to and after harvesting operations (chapter 3). These georeferenced vegetation samples provided an excellent opportunity to investigate the following questions:

---

[1] A summary of *A test of Airborne Laser Mapping Under Varying Forest Canopy* (Reutebuch et al. 2000).

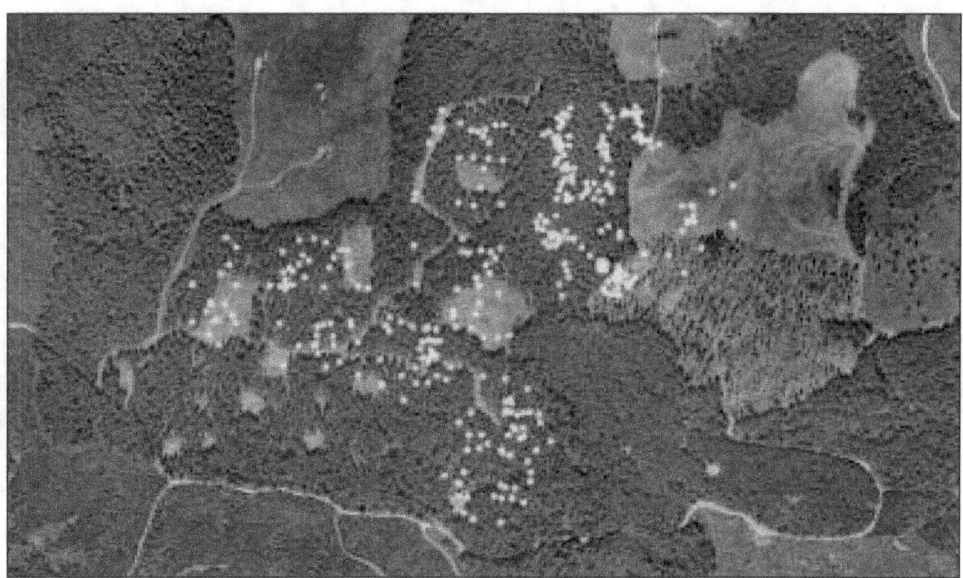

Figure 10-1—1999 orthophotograph of the LIDAR study area, after harvest. Yellow dots indicate the location of 350 ground survey checkpoints. (Washington State DNR, Resource Mapping Section.)

1. How accurately can LIDAR map the ground surface under varying canopy densities?

2. Can LIDAR data be used to measure stand and individual tree characteristics?

To investigate these questions, a LIDAR system was flown over the study area both prior to harvesting in 1998 and after harvesting in 1999. The instrument was a Saab Topeye[2] LIDAR system that was mounted in a helicopter and operated by Aerotec of Bessemer, Alabama. The LIDAR coverage area is mountainous with elevation varying from approximately 500 to 1,300 ft and ground slopes from 0 to 45 degrees.

Accuracy of LIDAR-Derived Digital Terrain Models Under Forest Canopy

The accuracy of two digital terrain models (DTMs) derived from the two LIDAR data sets was assessed (Reutebuch et al. 2000). Ground elevations from the airborne laser DTMs were compared to 350 ground survey points distributed throughout the Blue Ridge harvesting treatment units (fig. 10-1). The root mean square error of the 1999 DTM was 2.4 ft with an average error of 0.0 ft. The root mean square error of the 1998 DTM was 3.8 ft with an average error of +1.3 ft. This work is discussed in more detail by Reutebuch et al. (2003).

The 1999 airborne laser DTM also was compared to spot heights measured photogrammetrically from 1:12,000 aerial photos. In all, 992 photogrammetric heights were measured throughout the study area (fig. 10-2). The average difference from the 1999 LIDAR DTM was 0.0 ft, with a standard deviation of 6.0 ft. In relatively open areas, the photogrammetric heights compared very well with the LIDAR DTM elevations. Eighty-seven percent of the photogrammetric heights were within 10 ft of the corresponding LIDAR DTM elevations. In areas with very tall, dense canopy, the photogrammetric heights occasionally had large errors.

---

[2] The use of trade or firm names is for the convenience of the reader and does not imply endorsement by the USDA Forest Service of any product or service.

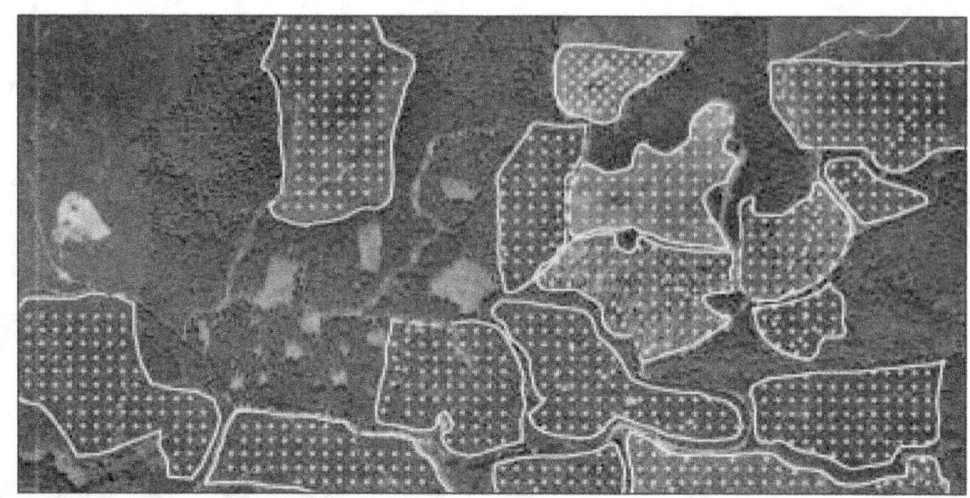

Figure 10-2—1999 orthophotograph showing location of 16 timber units in which photogrammetric spot heights were collected. Yellow dots represent spot heights in timber units. Red crosses represent spot heights on roads. (Washington State DNR, Resource Mapping Section.)

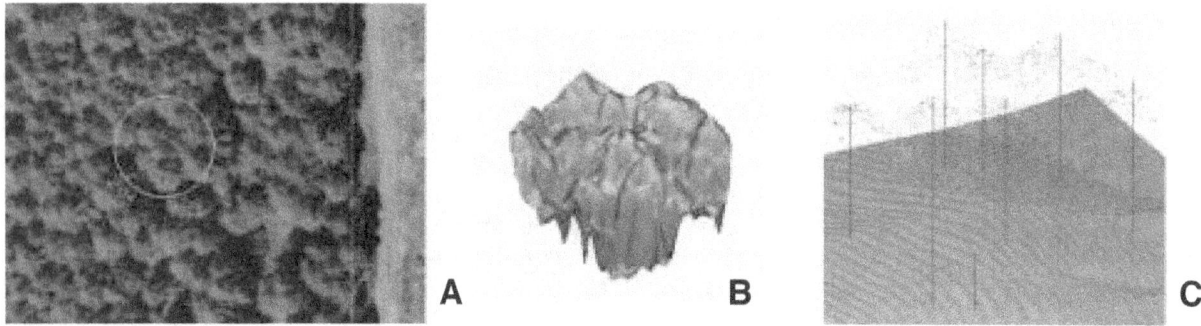

Figure 10-3—(a) Large-scale aerial photo showing growth plot, (b) detailed canopy surface model generated from LIDAR data, and (c) estimated individual tree stem locations and heights from LIDAR data.

LIDAR Measurement of Stand and Individual Tree Characteristics

In addition to assessing the accuracy of the LIDAR ground DTMs, methods are being developed to estimate both stand and individual tree metrics from the LIDAR data. Andersen et al. (2001) found that individual tree crown apexes in the overstory could be measured to within 2 m of photogrammetrically-measured tree tops. Individual trees evident on large-scale aerial photographs (fig. 10-3) were successfully detected by using LIDAR data with a "user's" accuracy of 89 percent (error of commission of 11 percent) and a "producer's" accuracy of 83 percent (error of omission of 17 percent). It appears that average stand height can be estimated well from LIDAR data; however, much work remains to determine if other metrics such as density, crown size, crown length, and diameter can be accurately estimated.

References

Andersen, H.E.; Reutebuch, S.E.; Schreuder, G.F. 2001. Automated individual tree management through morphological analysis of a LIDAR-based canopy surface model. In: Proceedings of the 1st International precision forestry cooperative symposium. Seattle, WA: College of Forest Resources, University of Washington: 11-22

Reutebuch, S.E.; Ahmed, K.M.; Curtis, T.A. [et al.]. 2000. A test of airborne laser mapping under varying forest canopy. In: Proceedings, ASPRS 2000. Bethesda, MD: American Society for Photogrammetry and Remote Sensing. 9 p.

Reutebuch, S.E.; McGaughey, R.J.; Anderson, H.E.; Carson, W.W. 2003. Accuracy of a high-resolution LIDAR terrain model under a conifer forest canopy. Canadian Journal of Remote Sensing. 29(5): 527-535.

Chapter 11: Overall Discussion and Conclusions

Robert O. Curtis, David D. Marshall, and Dean S. DeBell

Compared to the conventional clearcut, all other regimes in the experiment markedly reduced visual impacts after initial harvest, particularly when sites are viewed at low angles. The treatments have produced strongly contrasting stand structures, which should have a strong influence on future wildlife values and on stand growth, in addition to aesthetic values. At this early stage, we have as yet no growth information, and no conclusions can be drawn about differences in actual long-term yields (as opposed to simulation estimates that may be considerably in error).

Costs of implementation clearly differed. As would be expected, sale preparation and administration and harvesting costs per unit of timber output increased as volume removed decreased. We believe that all regimes included are feasible with ground-based harvesting systems; the Copper Ridge site will provide a test of feasibility with cable systems. Each regime might be desirable under some combination of circumstances and owner objectives. There is no single best regime.

A major element in cost of sale preparation was the cost of marking for thinning in both the continued thinning regime and in the matrix of the patch cut and group selection regimes. This was somewhat inflated by an inexperienced crew. More importantly, Washington Department of Natural Resources has been having considerable success with unmarked thinning by the contractor, which largely eliminates the marking cost and is the method being used at the Copper Ridge site. It should be possible to substantially reduce this element of the cost differences.

The Blue Ridge experiment was installed at stand age 69. Most of the area had one thinning at about age 42. The stand was therefore in comparatively vigorous condition. This fact may be related to the comparatively small windfall losses to date.

The initial stand, however, was considerably older than would be desirable as a starting point for conversion to the two-age, patch cut, and group selection regimes. By the time the planted trees in the two-age stand reach harvestable size, and by the time the conversion process is complete in the patch cut and group selection treatments, we will have produced some very large trees.

Although very large trees are beneficial to aesthetic and wildlife values, they could be a major drawback from the timber production standpoint despite their advantages in timber quality. With the current shift of many industrial and private owners to short-rotation management, and the near cessation of timber sales from federal lands, few mills remain that are capable of processing very large trees. Whether or not this will be a serious obstacle in the future will depend on whether or not such regimes are applied on a sufficient scale to maintain a processing capability for large trees. Such regimes should be very well suited to multiple use public lands such as the national forests, where there is strong pressure to develop stands with some of the characteristics associated with old growth.

Ideally, the two-age regime and conversion to the patch cut and group selection regimes should begin somewhere around age 40, rather than at 70 as at Blue Ridge. The third replicate in the planned Capitol Forest installations will approximate this, as will the Canadian replicate(s), discussed below, the first of which was established at age 55.

The economic analysis presented necessarily involves somewhat uncertain estimates of future yields and future dollar values, specific assumed rotations, and—in the case of Blue Ridge—treatments begun at an age older than would be desirable. Lacking long-term experience data for a number of these regimes, yield estimates are necessarily based on simulations involving assumptions that, although plausible, may not be correct. Comparisons among regimes also are somewhat clouded by differences in assumed rotations, which contribute to the estimated differences among regimes. (Time and personnel constraints prevented a thorough examination of the effect of rotation assumptions.) And, the analysis considers only timber values. Although returns from timber are the dominant consideration for some owners, in recent years timber values have become a subsidiary consideration for some public owners, and all owners are affected by conflicts with other values and societal objectives. These other values and objectives are necessarily excluded from the economic analysis, because there is no available basis for assigning dollar values. However, the analysis does provide some first estimates of the costs in reduced net present value of timber that are associated with management changes designed to meet these other objectives.

The LIDAR trials were superimposed on the study to take advantage of the existing plot data. They illustrate the fact that long-term studies of this kind provide opportunities for other research not necessarily related to the original objectives. The apparent ability of LIDAR to provide detailed information on topography and forest cover does suggest that it will probably have usefulness in locating and delineating suitable areas for future research studies.

This experiment has provided management experience with the use of alternative silvicultural regimes. It also provides examples of these alternatives that have already received much use as demonstration areas for foresters, students, and the interested public.

Beyond the work described in this report, the study offers opportunities for additional research and supplementary studies, dependent on availability of resources and cooperators. Notable examples include the following:

- Growth and yield. Growth and mortality of the residual stand, planted trees, and advance natural reproduction will be monitored, and growth responses to treatment, yields, and changes in stand structure will be compared.

- Evaluation of wildlife effects. Treatment units are large enough to permit evaluation of songbird and small mammal populations and use. Populations and use will change as regeneration develops, additional patches or groups are cut, and stand structures continue to change. Consequently, repeated measurements over an extended time are needed. The silviculture team does not have the needed expertise for wildlife evaluations; thus such work is dependent on cooperators.

- Public response. Appearance of stands will change markedly as they develop over time, and there is need for continuing evaluation. Again, this work is dependent on cooperation with others. Aside from research, these areas could also become a valuable educational resource.

- Soil effects. The limited work described above seems to indicate relatively little surface disturbance; no work has been done on other soil effects. There is opportunity for this at Blue Ridge and also at the installations of the associated overstory density study.

- Effects of edge and opening size on regeneration and shrub development. Data from the plot grid will provide overall unit estimates of regeneration development and stand growth and yield. In the patch cut and group selection regimes, however, such data probably will not be sufficient to evaluate effects of opening size on shrub competition and on tree species regeneration and growth. Supplementary transect sampling could provide valuable information.

- Additional replicates. Additional replication outside Capitol Forest could strengthen conclusions and expand the geographic range of inference. The Westside Silvicultural Options Team (Olympia) does not have the means to do this, but the British Columbia Ministry of Forests has established an additional replicate on Vancouver Island, with two more planned. The Canadian version is called the Silviculture Treatments for Ecosystem Management in the Sayward (STEMS) project and implements the six treatments according to the study protocol, plus an additional variable retention treatment.

In recent years, a number of large studies have been established in the Pacific Northwest dealing with alternatives to traditional clearcutting (Monserud 2002). The Capitol Forest study described here, however, differs from most others in that it compares widely contrasting silvicultural regimes applied over an extended period rather than single-entry treatments. Unlike most others, it also provides data on harvesting and management costs involved. Continuity is crucial to its success, both as a scientific experiment and as an increasingly valuable demonstration area both for foresters and for the general public.

Reference   **Monserud, R.A. 2002.** Large-scale management experiments in the moist maritime forests of the Pacific Northwest. Landscape and Urban Planning. 59: 159-180.

Metric Equivalents

When you know:	Multiply by:	To find:
Inches (in)	2.54	Centimeters (cm)
Feet (ft)	.3028	Meters (m)
Square feet (ft^2)	.0929	Square meters (m^2)
Cubic feet (ft^3)	.028	Cubic meters (m^3)
Acres (ac)	.4047	Hectares (ha)
Milacres	.0004047	Hectares (ha)
Square feet per acre (ft^2/ac)	.2296	Square meters per hectare (m^2/ha)
Cubic feet per acre (ft^3/ac)	.06997	Cubic meters per hectare (m^3/ha)
Miles per hour (mph)	1.609	Kilometers per hour (kph)
Fluid ounces (oz)	.0296	Liters (L)
Gallons (gal)	3.78	Liters (L)
Tons	.907	Megagrams (Mg)
Degrees Fahrenheit (°F)	(F-32) x 0.556	Degrees Celsius (°C)

Appendix A: Soil Description at Blue Ridge Site

John Shumway

Mapped as: Olympic Series, a fine, mixed, active, Palehumults.

The Olympic Series consists of very deep, well-drained soils formed in residuum weathered from basalt. This soil profile is located on a 20-percent east-facing slope at 1,000 ft (300 m) elevation.

The pedon at the site is as follows (colors are moist, and entire profile was moist when described):

Oi	2.5 to 0 in	Litter consisting of needles, twigs, and conifer branches.
A	0 to 9 in	Dark brown (7.5YR 3/2) silty clay loam; strong very fine and fine subangular blocky and fine granular structure; friable, slightly sticky and plastic; many roots; many fine pores; wavy boundary.
AB	9 to 15 in	Dark reddish-brown (5YR 3/4) silty clay loam; very fine and fine subangular blocky structure; friable, slightly sticky, and plastic; many fine roots; wavy boundary.
Bt1	15 to 28 in	Dark reddish-brown (5YR 3/4) silty clay loam; moderate medium fine subangular blocky structure; friable, slightly sticky, and plastic; common roots; gradual smooth boundary.
Bt2	28 to 33 in	Yellowish-red (5YR 5/5) silty clay; moderate coarse subangular blocky structure; friable, slightly sticky, and plastic; common roots; gradual smooth boundary.
Bt3	33 to 42 in	Yellowish-red (5YR 5/6) clay; moderate medium and fine subangular blocky structure; friable, slightly sticky, and plastic; few roots; gradual smooth boundary.
Bt4	106 to 165 in	Reddish-yellow (5YR 6/5) clay; moderate medium subangular blocky structure; firm, slightly sticky, and plastic; few roots; gradual smooth boundary.

Appendix B: Blue Ridge Vegetation Assessment

David Peter

The Blue Ridge vegetation assessment was based on two reconnaissance field visits on May 21 and June 13, 2000. Written notes were taken on site at each treatment unit. Visible areas were mapped on treatment maps and air photos. A plant association map was made in Arcview by interpolating field notes and maps and by extrapolating based on observed relationships between vegetation and topography (fig. B-1, tables B-1 and B-2). When plots were encountered, the plant association (Henderson et al. 1989) was noted, but no systematic effort was made to visit each plot. The exact placement of plant association lines on the map is a somewhat arbitrary cutoff of a continuum.

The plant species codes[1] used are as follows:

Code	Scientific name	Common name
ATFI	*Athyrium filix-femina* (L.) Roth	ladyfern
BENE2[2]	*Berberis nervosa* Pursh	Cascade Oregon grape
EQAR	*Equisetum arvense* L.	common horsetail
GASH	*Gaultheria shallon* Pursh	salal
LYAM3	*Lysichiton americanus* Hulten & St. John	skunk cabbage
OPHO	*Oplopanax horridus* Miq.	devils club
OXOR	*Oxalis oregana* Nutt.	Oregon oxalis
POMU	*Polystichum munitum* (Kalfuss) K. Presl	swordfern
TITR	*Tiarella trifoliata* L.	three-leaved foamflower
TSHE	*Tsuga heterophylla* (Raf.) Sarg.	western hemlock

[1] Species codes and names follow USDA Natural Resources Conservation Service. 2002. The PLANTS database, version 3.5. (http://plants.usda.gov). National Plant Data Center, Baton Rouge, LA 70874-4490.

[2] BENE2 = MAN2 (*Mahonia nervosa* (Pursh) Nutt.) in the PLANTS database.

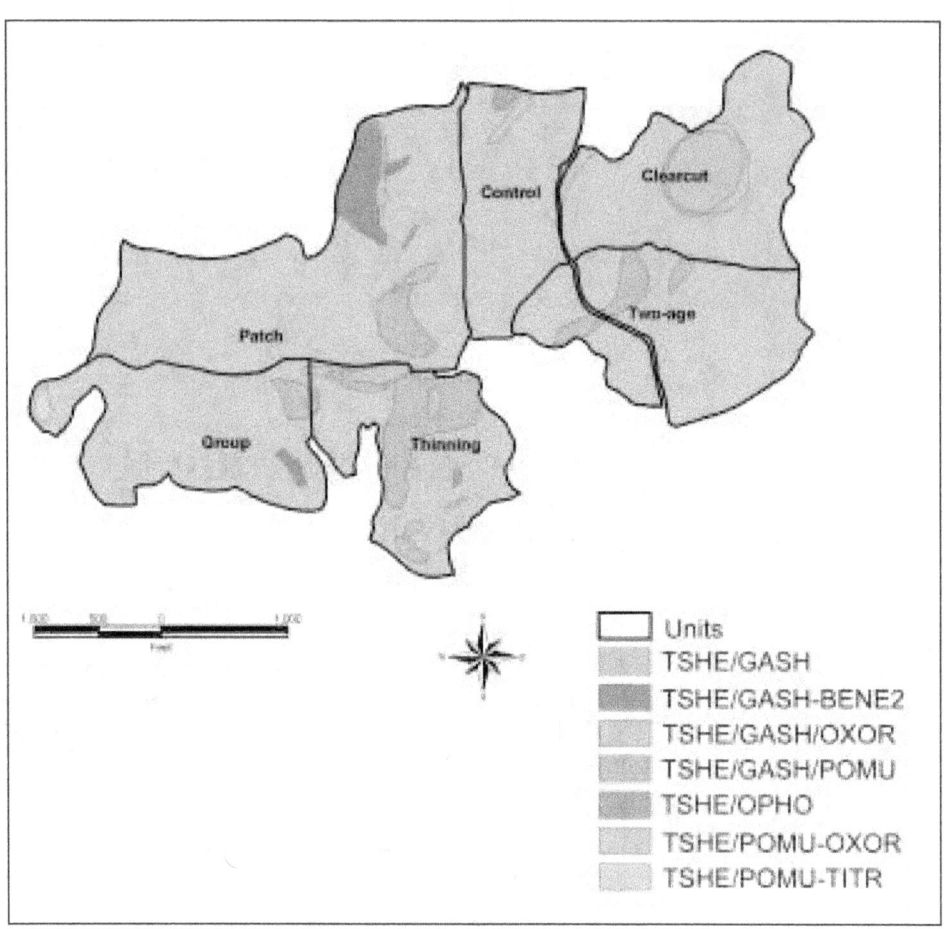

Figure B-1—Distribution of plant associations in the Blue Ridge study site. Species names are given in appendix B.

Table B-1—Plant association characteristics used to model unobserved areas for western hemlock series (TSHE)

Characteristic	POMU-OXOR	GASH/POMU	GASH	GASH/OXOR	GASH-BENE2	POMU/TITR	Wetlands
Aspect	All	SE-W	SE-W	SE-W	S-W	SE-SW	All
Relative soil depth	Moderately deep	Moderate	Shallow	Moderately shallow	Shallow	Moderately deep	Variable
Topographic position	Upper-lower slope	Ridge-upper slope	Ridge-upper slope	Ridge-upper slope	Ridge-upper slope	Midslope	Bottom
Slope shape	Straight-concave	Straight-convex	Convex	Straight-convex	Straight-convex	Straight-convex	Concave
Probable no. of plots	82	11	3	3	1	0	8

Table B-2—Identification numbers of plots assigned to plant associations other than POMU-OXOR, in the western hemlock series (TSHE)

	Clearcut	Two-age	Patch cut	Group selection	Repeated thinning	Control
GASH/POMU	8	1	8, 9, 15	7	5, 6, 10, 15	
GASH	7, 11				3	
GASH/OXOR	6, 12				16	
GASH-BENE2				20		
Wetlands		12		8, 16	14	5, 8, 9, 12

The TSHE/POMU-OXOR plant association dominates most of the Blue Ridge project area. Drier areas such as ridgetops, convex landforms, steep south-facing aspects, or areas with shallow soils have one of five drier plant associations. Wetter areas such as stream bottoms or areas with poor drainage have one of five wetter plant associations.

Successively drier plant associations are TSHE/POMU-OXOR, TSHE/GASH/OXOR, TSHE/GASH/POMU, and TSHE/GASH-BENE2. South aspects steeper than 35 percent are likely to be drier than TSHE/POMU-OXOR, but this depends on the distance from the top of the slope and slope shape. Areas mapped as TSHE/POMU-OXOR on or near ridgetops, convexities, and south or west aspects often are mosaics of two or more associations with a dominant matrix of TSHE/POMU-OXOR.

Sites wetter than TSHE/POMU-OXOR are TSHE/OPHO and nonforest sites dominated by OPHO, LYAM3, ATFI, and EQAR. Collectively these are referred to as wetlands in table B-2. All sites wetter than TSHE/POMU-OXOR were riparian along streams or seeps. Streams with channels as small as 1 meter wide have wetland riparian zones 3 to 4 meters wide. Typically LYAM3 or ATFI is on the banks or in the channel, with OPHO on the banks or slightly higher. Larger patches of OPHO occur in areas of seepage.

Many plots include portions of more than one plant association. This is always the case with wetlands. All the wetlands are too small to encompass an entire plot, so assignments to the wetland category in the tables only imply a wetland influence on part of the plot. Some upland plots also have more than one plant association. In these cases the plots have been placed in the dominant plant association category.

Reference

Henderson, J.A.; Peter, D.H.; Lesher, R.D.; Shaw, D.C. 1989. Forested plant associations of the Olympic National Forest. Ecol. Tech. Pap. R6-ECOL-TP-001-88. Portland, OR: U.S. Department of Agriculture, Forest Service, Pacific Northwest Region. 502 p.

Appendix C: Pretreatment and Posttreatment Stand Statistics by Species Group

Table C-1 presents pretreatment and posttreatment stand summaries by major species and minor species groups for the Blue Ridge treatment units. The summaries represent the average from the systematic grid of research plots located in each unit. Values are calculated from standing tree measurements on the permanent plots and will not be in complete agreement with values based on log scale and areas that include road right-of-ways.

Values for numbers of trees, basal area, and volume per acre are for live trees 5.6 inches and larger. Volumes are gross values without any defect deductions. Conifer volumes were computed for each tree by using the taper equations of Flewelling (1994). Volumes for hardwoods were computed by using the tarif system (Brackett 1973, Chambers and Foltz 1979). Heights for unmeasured trees were estimated by using height-diameter curves fit for each treatment by species group.

References

Brackett, M. 1973. Notes on tarif tree volume computation. Resour. Manage. Rep. 24. Olympia, WA: Washington Department of Natural Resources. 26 p.

Chambers, C.J.; Foltz, B.W. 1979. The tarif system—revisions and additions. DNR Rep. 27. Olympia, WA: Washington Department of Natural Resources. 8 p.

Flewelling, J.W. 1994. Stem form equation development notes. Northwest Taper Cooperative. Unpublished report. On file with: James Flewelling, 26724 51st Place S, Kent, WA 98032.

Table C-1—Pretreatment and posttreatment summary values[a] by species and species groups at Blue Ridge

Species[b]	Trees	Basal area	QMD[c]	CVTS[d]	CV6[e]	SV632[f]
	Number per acre	Square feet per acre	Inches	Cubic feet per acre		Board feet per acre
Clearcut pretreatment–16 plots						
DF	65.3	173.5	22.1	8,649	8,405	41,464
WH	37.5	41.4	14.2	2,020	1,879	8,526
OC	.6	.5	11.6	21	19	83
HW	10.6	11.6	14.2	550	505	2,378
Total	114.1	226.9	19.1	11,240	10,803	52,451
Two-age pretreatment–16 plots						
DF	83.1	202.2	21.1	10,102	9,802	47,669
WH	24.7	30.4	15.0	1,499	1,405	6,382
OC	1.9	1.0	10.1	45	38	173
HW	7.8	7.1	12.9	315	283	1,268
Total	117.5	240.8	19.4	11,961	11,528	55,492
Two-age posttreatment–16 plots						
DF	14.7	44.9	23.7	2,323	2,266	11,306
WH	.6	1.2	18.7	58	55	240
OC	.3	.2	9.7	5	4	16
HW	0	0	0	0	0	0
Total	15.6	46.3	23.3	2,386	2,325	11,562
Patches pretreatment–26 plots						
DF	57.3	117.6	23.8	8,948	8,723	43,849
WH	33.3	43.3	15.5	2,141	2,012	9,318
OC	2.7	3.5	15.5	167	155	728
HW	4.6	6.5	16.1	322	301	1,488
Total	97.9	231.0	20.8	11,578	11,191	55,383

Table C-1—Pretreatment and posttreatment summary values[a] by species and species groups at Blue Ridge (continued)

Species[b]	Trees	Basal area	QMD[c]	CVTS[d]	CV6[e]	SV632[f]
	Number per acre	Square feet per acre	Inches	Cubic feet per acre		Board feet per acre
Patches posttreatment–26 plots						
DF	39.4	137.1	25.3	6,873	6,711	34,066
WH	11.5	21.3	18.4	1,080	1,028	4,822
OC	1.0	1.0	13.5	29	26	96
HW	.6	.8	15.5	35	33	155
Total	52.5	160.1	23.6	8,017	7,798	39,139
Groups pretreatment–19 plots						
DF	78.7	220.0	22.6	11,051	10,752	53,663
WH	12.1	12.6	13.8	595	549	2,478
OC	5.3	2.8	9.9	122	100	429
HW	5.5	3.6	11.0	151	125	579
Total	101.6	239.0	20.8	11,919	11,526	57,149
Groups posttreatment–19 plots						
DF	41.6	133.6	24.3	6,867	6,701	33,876
WH	1.0	.6	10.3	15	11	30
OC	0	0	0	0	0	0
HW	0	0	0	0	0	0
Total	42.6	134.2	24.0	6,882	6,712	33,906
Thinning pretreatment–16 plots						
DF	105.9	235.0	20.2	11,749	11,374	54,846
WH	5.3	1.9	8.0	54	35	126
OC	1.6	.9	10.5	41	36	153
HW	16.3	17.0	13.9	780	716	3,266
Total	129.1	254.9	19.0	12,624	12,161	58,391

Table C-1—Pretreatment and posttreatment summary values[a] by species and species groups at Blue Ridge (continued)

Species[b]	Trees	Basal area	QMD[c]	CVTS[d]	CV6[e]	SV632[f]
	Number per acre	*Square feet per acre*	*Inches*	*Cubic feet per acre*		*Board feet per acre*
Thinning posttreatment–16 plots						
DF	68.1	189.1	22.6	9,659	9,404	46,487
WH	0.6	0.2	7.0	3	1	0
OC	0.6	0.6	13.4	14	12	33
HW	1.9	2.6	15.8	127	119	580
Total	71.3	192.4	22.3	9,803	9,536	47,100
Control–15 plots						
DF	40.3	147.6	25.9	7,807	7,635	39,683
WH	50.0	90.1	18.2	4,749	4,532	21,876
OC	12.0	12.2	13.7	464	421	1,787
HW	9.7	11.2	14.6	557	518	2,446
Total	112.0	261.2	20.7	13,577	13,106	65,792

[a] Values exclude area in reserves and roads.
[b] Species: DF = Douglas-fir, WH = western hemlock, OC = other conifers, and HW = hardwoods.
[c] QMD: Quadratic mean diameter.
[d] CVTS: Total stem cubic-foot volume.
[e] CV6: Merchantable cubic-foot volume to a 6-inch top diameter inside bark.
[f] SV632: Scribner board-foot volume to a 6-inch top diameter inside bark in 32-foot logs.
Source: Flewelling 1994.

www.ingramcontent.com/pod-product-compliance
Lightning Source LLC
Chambersburg PA
CBHW080300290526

45790CB00005B/1879